Cambridge Elements ≡

Elements in the Philosophy of Ludwig Wittgenstein
edited by
David G. Stern
University of Iowa

WITTGENSTEIN ON ASPECT PERCEPTION

Avner Baz
Tufts University, Massachusetts

CAMBRIDGE
UNIVERSITY PRESS

CAMBRIDGE
UNIVERSITY PRESS

University Printing House, Cambridge CB2 8BS, United Kingdom

One Liberty Plaza, 20th Floor, New York, NY 10006, USA

477 Williamstown Road, Port Melbourne, VIC 3207, Australia

314–321, 3rd Floor, Plot 3, Splendor Forum, Jasola District Centre,
New Delhi – 110025, India

79 Anson Road, #06–04/06, Singapore 079906

Cambridge University Press is part of the University of Cambridge.

It furthers the University's mission by disseminating knowledge in the pursuit of
education, learning, and research at the highest international levels of excellence.

www.cambridge.org
Information on this title: www.cambridge.org/9781108813150
DOI: 10.1017/9781108878012

First published 2020

A catalogue record for this publication is available from the British Library.

ISBN 978-1-108-81315-0 Paperback
ISSN 2632-7112 (online)
ISSN 2632-7104 (print)

Wittgenstein on Aspect Perception

Elements in the Philosophy of Ludwig Wittgenstein

DOI: 10.1017/9781108878012
First published online: November 2020

Avner Baz
Tufts University, Massachusetts
Author for correspondence: Avner Baz, avner.baz@tufts.edu

Abstract: The perception of what he calls 'aspects' preoccupied Wittgenstein and gave him considerable trouble in his final years. The Wittgensteinian aspect defies any number of traditional philosophical dichotomies: the aspect is neither subjective (inner, metaphysically private) nor objective; it presents perceivable unity and sense that are (arguably) not (yet) conceptual; it is 'subject to the will', but at the same time is normally taken to be genuinely revelatory of the object perceived under it. This Elemént begins with a grammatical and phenomenological characterization of Wittgensteinian aspects. It then challenges two widespread ideas: that aspects are to be identified with concepts, and that aspect perception has a continuous version that is characteristic of (normal) human perception. It concludes by proposing that aspect perception brings to light the distinction between the world *as perceived* and the world *as objectively construed*, and the role we play in the constitution of the *former*.

Keywords: Wittgenstein; Perception; Aspect Perception; Phenomenology; Philosophical Method

ISBNs: 9781108813150 (PB), 9781108878012 (OC)
ISSNs: 2632-7112 (online), 2632-7104 (print)

Contents

Introduction

The following monograph draws on, and from, work on aspect perception that I've done over the past twenty years or so and published in eight papers that are very different from each other – not only in terms of their focus and emphases, but also in terms of their perspective and approach. For a while, I had toyed with the idea of turning my work on aspects into a monograph but was reluctant to do so, fearing that the dialectical nature of the work – the ways in which it is tied to particular conversations with particular interlocutors and rooted in particular moments of my philosophical development and the particular interests of those moments – would thereby be distorted. Now that the eight papers – all more or less substantively revised and expanded from their originally published version – have come out in a collection (Baz 2020), I have felt ready to do the exercise of distilling my work on aspects into this short monograph on Wittgenstein on aspect perception, which I hope the readers will find useful. I do feel that thirty years after the publication of Stephen Mulhall's insightful and rightfully influential *On Being in the World: Wittgenstein and Heidegger on Seeing Aspects*, the philosophical discussion of aspect perception – in Wittgenstein and more generally – stands in need of refocusing. Only time will tell whether this short monograph succeeds in refocusing it – if only by provoking others to articulate their disagreements with it. But I am, in any case, grateful to David Stern and to Cambridge University Press for the invitation to write it.

The aim of this Element is to introduce readers to what the later Wittgenstein calls "aspects", and to some of the most basic questions that have arisen in the literature about Wittgensteinian aspects and their significance.[1]

Section 1 will offer both a *grammatical* characterization and a *phenomenological* characterization of Wittgensteinian aspects. It will be emphasized that though Wittgenstein himself was suspicious of phenomenology and sometimes even presented his grammatical investigation as an antidote to what he saw as the pitfalls of phenomenology, both sorts of characterization are important for an understanding of what he calls "aspects", and for a proper appreciation of the significance of aspect perception.

Section 2 will challenge the widespread tendency – exhibited by Strawson, Wollheim, and others – to identify Wittgensteinian aspects with, or in terms of, *concepts*. It will be argued that on any of the most common ways of understanding "concept", or our concept of *concept*, that identification is misguided, and distorts both the grammar and the phenomenology of aspect perception. The

---

[1] I speak of *Wittgensteinian* aspects, because I believe that the perception of what Wittgenstein calls "aspects" – even though it takes a variety of forms and manifests itself in a variety of contexts – is more specific than what some of his interpreters have made it out to be.

basic point will be that Wittgensteinian aspects are *not general* as concepts essentially are and are *not separable* from the objects perceived under them in the way that concepts are.

In Section 3, I will propose that while not having the generality of concepts, and while being inseparable – grammatically and phenomenologically – from the things perceived under them, Wittgensteinian aspects nonetheless connect the things perceived under them with other things. The connection, I will propose, is perceptual and internal, in the sense that how one thing presents itself to us perceptually – its perceived "physiognomy" – is not separable from its perceived relation to other things.

Sections 4 and 5 will address the idea – to be found in Strawson, Wollheim, Mulhall, Searle, and others – that there is a *continuous* version to the perception of aspects, and that, indeed, all (normal) human perception may aptly be understood as the perception of aspects. It will be argued in Section 4 that the textual basis for attributing that idea to Wittgenstein is weak, and that there is much textual evidence against that attribution. The idea of continuous aspect perception, it will then be argued in Section 5, fails to recognize the *indeterminacy* of the phenomenal world – by which I mean, the world *as perceived and responded to* prior to being *thought*, or thought or talked *about*, and so prior to being *conceptualized*. The dawning of Wittgensteinian aspects, whether solicited or unsolicited, willed or unwilled, it will be proposed, is the necessarily passing introduction of (relative) determinacy into the phenomenal world – a momentary taking hold of things, perceptually.

Section 6 will address the question of the significance of aspect perception: what, if anything, does the perception of Wittgensteinian aspects reveal about (normal) human perception *as such*? It will be proposed that it reveals the role we play in bringing about and sustaining the unity and sense of the phenomenal world; and it also reveals our capacity for more or less playful, more or less creative, projection of perceivable sense onto some given object, or situation.

In the Appendix, I will say something about what I see as the limitations of the Wittgensteinian grammatical investigation, as those limitations make themselves manifest in Wittgenstein's remarks on aspects.

1 The Grammar and Phenomenology of Wittgensteinian Aspects

I begin with what I take Wittgenstein to mean by "seeing (perceiving) something as something" or "seeing (perceiving) an aspect". The first few remarks of Section xi of part II of the *Investigations* are a good place to seek initial orientation:

Two uses of the word "see".

The one: "What do you see there?" – "I see *this*" (and then a description, a drawing, a copy). The other: "I see a likeness between these two faces" – where the man I say this to may be seeing the faces as clearly as I do myself.

The importance of this is the difference in category between the two 'objects' of sight.

The one man might make an accurate drawing of the two faces, and the other notice in the drawing the likeness which the former did not see.

I contemplate a face, and then suddenly notice its likeness to another. I *see* that it has not changed; and yet I see it differently. I call this experience "noticing an aspect" (Wittgenstein 2009b (hereafter 'PPF'), 111–3, translation amended).

The first thing to note, even before we draw on the basis of these remarks an understanding of what Wittgenstein means by "seeing-as" or by "aspect", is that he characterizes his subject matter both *grammatically* – in the Wittgensteinian sense of that term – and *phenomenologically*. On the one hand, he talks about two *uses of the word* "see", and gives an initial and partial characterization of those two uses. This is in line with his later philosophical practice. At the root of any number of traditional philosophical difficulties, Wittgenstein identified the tendency to suppose that our words – including philosophically troublesome words such as "see", "understand", "know", "think", "mean", "intend", "pain", and so on – 'name objects', or, as contemporary analytic philosophers like to say, 'refer to (denote) items in the world'; and accordingly to suppose that the best way to become clear about the meaning of those words, or the concepts they embody, is to identify and study those 'objects' directly – that is, not by way of an investigation of the use of those words.[2] What Wittgenstein tries to get us to see is that the model, or picture, of 'object and designation' (Wittgenstein 2009a (hereafter 'PI'), 293) is misguided and misleading when it comes to such words, and that what we end up producing, when we attempt to elucidate the nature of the "objects" to which they are supposed to refer, are philosophically constructed chimeras – 'structures of air', as he puts it (PI, 118) – that we erect by the light of questionable or confused theoretical commitments, and on the basis of 'pictures' that we have formed for ourselves of those "objects".

Wittgenstein's appeal to the *use* of philosophically troublesome words, or to what he calls their 'grammar', is an antidote to the tendencies and the

---

[2] In Baz (2017a), I argue, following Wittgenstein and Merleau-Ponty, against this prevailing conception of language, which (I argue) has underwritten the philosophical "method of cases" and hence a significant portion of the work produced within mainstream analytic philosophy in the past fifty years or so.

philosophical idleness or emptiness they lead to. In the remarks on aspects, he repeatedly urges his reader (or himself) not to try to understand aspect perception by way of introspection of what happens in or to us when we see an aspect (see PPF, 241; and Wittgenstein 1980a (hereafter 'RPPI'), 1011). '*Forget*', he urges his reader (or himself), 'forget that you have these experiences yourself' (Wittgenstein 1980b (hereafter 'RPPII', 531). 'Don't try to analyze the experience within yourself' (PPF, 188; see also PPF, 204). 'The question', he writes, 'is not *what happens here* [that is, when someone tells me: "Now I am seeing *this* point as the apex of the triangle", AB], but rather: how one may use that statement' (RPPI, 315). Wittgenstein reorients his reader's attention away from his or her own experience and toward the use of relevant words – here, first and foremost, the words with which the experience of noticing an aspect may aptly and naturally be voiced. To attain clarity about the seeing of aspects – or for that matter about any other 'concept of experience (*Erfahrungsbegriff*)' (PPF, 115) – we need to do more than just remind ourselves of particular isolated forms of words that may be used to describe or otherwise give voice to our experience. We need also to remind ourselves of 'the occasion and purpose' of these phrases (PPF, 311). 'It is necessary to get down to the application' (PPF, 165), to ask oneself 'What does anyone tell me by saying "Now I see it as ... "? What consequences has this piece of communication? What can I do with it?' (PPF, 176, translation amended). In my experience, commentators on Wittgenstein's remarks on aspect perception have tended to lose contact with his subject matter, and to get themselves confused, as a result of failing to heed this Wittgensteinian call altogether. The use of the relevant terms, and the language-game(s) within which they have their sense, have often been neglected in favor of theoretical commitments and ambitions, which are often sustained by misleading pictures.[3]

Before offering a grammatical characterization of Wittgensteinian aspects, I must note that Wittgenstein introduces the notion of "aspect" by way of the experience of *noticing* an aspect, of suddenly *being struck* by an aspect. And it might be tempting to suppose, as any number of readers of Wittgenstein's remarks on aspects have supposed, that Wittgensteinian aspects may also be, and regularly are, perceived continuously, and that Wittgenstein finds the experience of aspect *dawning* or *lighting up* interesting, and focuses on it, only because it brings to light in a dramatic fashion the reality of continuous

---

[3] Thus, for example, Severin Schroeder writes: '[W]henever something is seen (and not only looked at inanely or absent-mindedly) *some* aspect of it must be noticed, be it only certain shapes or colours' (2010, 366). But how exactly, or in what sense, is the color of an object or its shape an *aspect*? Surely not in Wittgenstein's sense. And why are aspects, *thus* understood, philosophically interesting?

aspect perception as our normal perceptual relation to things.[4] As against this common reading of Wittgenstein, I will argue, in Section 4, that Wittgensteinian aspects can *only dawn*, as he himself puts it. An aspect is perceived only as long as we attend to the object in a particular way; and our attention is, at least normally, shifting and unstable. For this reason, the following grammatical elucidation of Wittgensteinian aspects is a grammatical elucidation of *dawning* aspects; it follows Wittgenstein's express aim of elucidating the concept of *noticing an aspect* and *its* place 'among the concepts of experience' (PPF, 115).

What then can we say about the grammar of (dawning) Wittgensteinian aspects? Taking our initial bearing from the opening remarks of PPF, section xi, cited at the opening of this section, we could say at least the following. To begin with, aspects are contrasted with 'objects of sight' of a different 'category'. What are these *other* objects of sight? A red circle over there would be one example (PPF, 121), a knife and a fork would be another example (PPF, 122), a conventional picture of a lion yet another (PPF, 203). Another type of object of sight that Wittgenstein contrasts with aspects is 'a property of the object' (PPF, 247). In short, aspects contrast with what is objectively there to be seen, where what is objectively there to be seen may be determined, and *known* to be there, from a third-person perspective, and independently of any(one's) particular perceptual *experience* of it. In contrast, someone may look at an object, see everything there is to see about it – in the first, objective sense of "see" – and yet fail to see (second sense) an aspect that may be seen by another. For this reason, it may aptly be said that aspects 'teach us nothing about the external world' (RPPI, 899). This last remark, while illuminating, has to be taken with caution, however, for it is going to matter what one understands by "teaching something" and by "the external world". In particular, the tendency to think that if the aspect is not objective (part or feature of "the external world" objectively understood) it must be subjective ("inner", metaphysically private) needs to be resisted; for it may be that one important lesson to be learned from the phenomenon, or set of related phenomena, of aspect perception is precisely that this traditional dichotomy is at least sometimes misguided and misleading. Given the common philosophical understanding of "objective" and "subjective", or "external" and "internal", the Wittgensteinian aspect is, importantly, neither: it is genuinely perceived, and sharable with others, but, at the same time, is not independent of its perceivers, or of its being perceived. In this, I will propose in

---

[4] This particular reading of Wittgenstein was first proposed in Stephen Mulhall's influential *On Being in the World: Wittgenstein and Heidegger on Seeing Aspects* (Mulhall 1990); but the idea that "continuous aspect perception" characterizes normal human perception may already be found in Peter Strawson's 'Imagination and Perception' (Strawson 1982 (1971)). The idea may also be found in Richard Wollheim's *Art and Its Objects* (1980). It will be discussed in Sections 4 and 5.

Section 6, the aspect announces the phenomenal world, and its distinction from the world as objectively construed.

The objects of sight with which aspects contrast may be described and often will be described (or otherwise represented) in order to *inform* someone else who for some reason is not in a position to see (or otherwise perceive) them – in order to teach her, precisely, something about the world as it is independently of any (particular person's) *experience* of it. The other person, in Wittgenstein's remark, asks 'What do you see *there*?'; and unless she is testing our eyesight or linguistic competence, she is asking because she cannot, for some more or less contingent reason, see for herself. By contrast, the person with whom we seek to share what we see when we see an aspect would normally be standing there with us and seeing as clearly as we do the object (the face, for example) in which we see the aspect (its likeness to some other face). Indeed, as Wittgenstein says, she could even make an (objectively) accurate representation of the object while failing to see the aspect.

In giving voice to the seeing of an aspect, we accordingly normally seek, not to 'inform the other person' but rather, as Wittgenstein puts it, to come in contact with, or 'find', the other (RPPI, 874). In everyday, natural contexts – as opposed to the artificial ones of the lab or classroom – the seeing of aspects makes for a particular type of opportunity for seeking intimacy with others, or putting it to the test. Like beauty, at least as understood by Kant in the *Critique of the Power of Judgment*, Wittgensteinian aspects are importantly characterized by the possibility that a fully competent speaker (and perceiver) may fail to see (or otherwise perceive) them even though she sees (first sense) as well as anyone else the objects in which they are seen, and by the particular sense it makes to *call upon* such a person to see them.[5]

This last point is connected with another feature of aspects: their being 'subject to the will' (see RPPI, 899 and 976; and RPPII, 545). Wittgensteinian aspects are subject to the will not so much, or primarily, in the sense that we can see them at will, but precisely in the sense that it makes sense both to call upon another person to see them and to *try* to see this or that particular aspect (PPF, 256). In the natural course of everyday experience, however, Wittgensteinian aspects normally dawn on us uninvited – except for when the invitation comes from another person – and even, sometimes, against our will (LWI, 612). They strike us. And yet we know *we* had something to do with their dawning, for we know that the objective world – the world that may be defined by its independence from any(one's) particular experience of it – has not changed, and that no new element of *that* world was revealed to us in the dawning of the aspect. In

[5] Cf. Kant (2000), Prussian Academy Edition page numbers 211–19 and 279ff.

this way, I will later suggest, the dawning of Wittgensteinian aspects reveals that the world as pre-reflectively perceived and responded to is not the world as thought (or talked) about in objective terms.

So much, for now, by way of grammatical characterization of what Wittgenstein calls 'aspects'. All of this Wittgensteinian grammar notwithstanding, the dawning (or noticing) of a Wittgensteinian aspect – unlike thinking, or knowing, or intending, or understanding, or meaning, or reading, or following ... this or that – *is*, first and foremost and essentially, a perceptual *experience* with a distinct phenomenology. Wittgenstein in no way denies this – indeed, that the dawning of a Wittgensteinian aspect is a particular sort of perceptual experience is *part of its grammar* (cf. PPF, 113). The later Wittgenstein was, however, generally suspicious of phenomenology, and skeptical of its capacity to lead to philosophical enlightenment. As I've already noted, this suspicion and skepticism comes out clearly and explicitly in his remarks on aspects, when he calls upon his readers to forget that they have such experiences themselves and to think about aspect perception from a third-person perspective. As I have already noted, and as I have argued at length elsewhere,[6] Wittgenstein's mistrust of phenomenology, and the shift to the third-person perspective, are well motivated, and serve him well, when it comes to the sorts of concepts, and phenomena, on which he focuses in the first part of the *Investigations*: understanding, learning, meaning (one's words one way or another), thinking, naming, reading, following a rule, intending, and so on; and they are also useful in elucidating the *concept* of (noticing an) aspect and its place among our concepts of experience. But, for reasons that will be discussed in the Appendix, I believe that Wittgenstein's general approach serves him less well, and sometimes leads him astray, when it comes to the *experience* of aspect dawning and its relation to other moments, features, and dimensions of our perceptual experience. The philosophical danger of being misled, or handicapped, by confining oneself to Wittgensteinian grammar is no less real, I believe, than the danger of getting confused, and lost, as result of its neglect. When it comes to aspect perception and to perception more generally, the Wittgensteinian grammatical-conceptual investigation should be complemented by properly executed phenomenology, and vice versa. And, as Merleau-Ponty has taught us, the phenomenal world is not private or inner; and the phenomenological recovery and elucidation of pre-reflective perceptual experience, even as it aims to recover and elucidate *our* perceptual experience, need not be based on *introspection* (Merleau-Ponty 1996/

---

[5] Baz (2011).

2012, 57/57–8)[7] – of which Wittgenstein was rightly suspicious – but may rather proceed on the basis of well-established empirical findings (cf. PP, 57/ 58 and 72/74). That we see something under *this* rather than *that* aspect, for example, or that a new aspect has just dawned on us, will normally show in how we respond to the thing and conduct ourselves in relation to it. And if someone cannot effect aspect-shifts for themselves – as Wittgenstein's 'aspect-blind', and many on the autistic spectrum, cannot – that too will show in their behavior, and will have far-reaching, empirically establishable consequences.

The phenomenology of noticing an aspect is fairly easy to give an initial characterization of, though no characterization would be much good to anyone not already familiar with the experience, and any form of words with which the experience might be characterized could also be understood in such ways that it would not aptly characterize the experience. When we notice an aspect, every- thing changes and yet nothing changes (see RPPII, 474). We *see* (in the objective sense of that word, the first of the two uses of it that Wittgenstein speaks of) that the object has not changed, and yet we see it differently (in what Wittgenstein refers to as the second use of "see"). We know, and see (first sense), that the object's objective features have remained unchanged, but its perceived physiognomy or overall expression *has* changed for us, and changed *wholly*. Aspect dawning thus brings out the *gestalt*, or *holistic*, nature of the world as pre-reflectively perceived – the internal relation between its elements, wherein the perceived significance of any element of the perceptual field is not independent of the perceived significance of other elements, and of the per- ceived significance of the whole. I'll say more about this in Section 3.

There is an important sense in which the aspect – unlike an objective property of the object – is *un-detachable* from the experience, or from the object-*as- experienced*.[8] Another way of putting that point, which will become important for us later on, is that to perceive an object under an aspect is not the same as applying a concept to it, which, being *general*, *is* separate from the particular object and from our particular experience of it. Objects of sight of the first category, Wittgenstein tells us, can be described (or otherwise represented) objectively: I may tell you that what I see is a knife and fork, or that the object I see is red, and thereby tell you exactly what I see – in the first sense of "see";

---

[7] References to the *Phenomenology of Perception* will henceforth be given by 'PP', with the page number of the pre-2002 editions of the Colin Smith translation, followed (as in the present case) by the page number of the 2012 Donald Landes translation. I will mostly be following the Smith's translation, amending it in accordance with Landes's translation whenever the latter seems superior.
[8] This, I suggest in Baz (2011), is why Wittgenstein found aspect perception useful for elucidating the "intransitive" sense, as he calls it, of "a quite particular", in the *Brown Book*.

and, if all goes well, you may thereby come to know *what* I see (first sense) as well as I do, and to be able to rightfully inform others about that object, even though you have not yourself perceived it. By contrast, if you want to know what I see when I see a Wittgensteinian aspect, or see some *x as y*, you need to look at *x* – or anyway at *some x* – and see *it* as *y* (or *recall* the experience of seeing some *x* as *y*). In this way, Wittgensteinian aspects illustrate what Merleau-Ponty describes as a physiognomic meaning, or sense, that *clings* what has it (PP, 147/148). In Section 6, I will suggest that it is precisely in bringing out, or dramatizing, *that* level of pre-conceptual, pre-objective sense-perception, that the dawning of Wittgensteinian aspects reveals something fundamental about human (and possibly not just human) perception. I will also say why that level of perception is not aptly thought of as continuous aspect perception.

The grammatical-phenomenological characterization I have just given of Wittgensteinian aspects is fairly specific; and yet it allows for quite a range of cases that differ from each other in more or less significant ways. Let me mention some of them: seeing a similarity between two faces, or some face *as* some other; seeing the duck-rabbit as a duck or as a rabbit; seeing a figure such as the famous Necker cube as oriented one way or another in space, relative to the perceiver; seeing the double-cross as a white cross against a black background, or vice versa; seeing a triangle – either drawn or "real" (three-dimensional) – as pointing in this or that direction, or as hanging from its apex, or as having fallen over ... (PPF, 162); seeing a face in a puzzle-picture; seeing a sphere in a picture as floating in the air (PPF, 169); seeing a W as an upside-down M and seeing the letter F as facing right, or left (see RPPII, 464–5); there's the aspect we may be said to see when something strikes us in a picture of a running horse and we exclaim 'It's running!' (RPPI, 874; see also PPF, 175); hearing a piece of music as plaintive (PPF, 229) or as solemn (PPF, 233), or hearing a bar as an introduction (PPF, 178); there is the experience in which 'everything strikes us as unreal' (RPPI, 125–6), which may be taken to represent a whole range of what could be called "aspects of mood"; and one could think of other sorts of perceptual "objects" that seem to fit the grammatical-phenomenological characterization I have given of Wittgensteinian aspects.

One important thing to note is that in some of the cases, the aspect corresponds to no objective judgment – what the object is seen *as* is not something that (in a different context perhaps) it could be seen, or known, to *be*. What, for example, would it be, or mean, for the letter F to *objectively be* facing right, or left? Moreover, even where we could think of an objective judgment that might be thought to correspond to the aspect – given a suitable context, the duck-rabbit could actually serve as a picture of a rabbit, or of a duck, and the Necker cube could be (meant to be taken as) an illustration of a cube going *this* (rather than that) way; a triangular wooden block that stands on its longest side could actually have fallen over (it might be that it is *supposed* to stand on its shortest side), and a drawn triangle might (be meant to) represent a triangle that has fallen over; there might actually *be* an objectively establishable similarity between two faces; and so on – no such judgment need be made by the perceiver of the aspect; and in the typical case, the perceiver of the aspect makes it clear that what she sees the object *as* is *not* necessarily something that she takes it to *be*. This is why we normally *invite* the other to see the aspect, and why we do not take her to be *mistaken* (or literally blind) if she cannot see the aspect we see. This is going to matter when we examine, in Section 2, the recurrent idea that aspects may be identified with, or in terms of, empirical concepts.

Another important thing to note is that aspects may be seen in non-ambiguous figures: for an aspect to dawn on us, there need not be, and often there is not, two (or more) competing, determinate aspects under which the object may be seen. This is one place where over-focusing on ambiguous figures such as the duck-rabbit or the Necker cube has led some readers of Wittgenstein astray, it seems to me. There is no clear, determinate aspect that competes with the similarity of one face to another, for example, and which that similarity, when it strikes us, might plausibly be thought to have replaced. Similarly, if you ask me to look at a face – whether depicted, photographed, or flesh and blood – and describe (what strikes me as) its expression, and I do, that does not mean that whenever I look at that or any other face, I see it as having some determinate expression or another. And even in cases where it seems that there are two or more determinate aspects under which an object may be seen, that does not mean that we must be seeing that object under one of them whenever we look at that object. For example, if you invite me to see, and say, which way the letter F is facing, and I look and it strikes me that it is facing right (say), that does *not* mean that *every time* I see the letter F I see it as facing right, or else as facing left. This will become important for us in Sections 4 and 5, when we ask what sense can be given to the recurrent idea that all (normal) seeing is seeing-as – that everything we see, at least normally, is seen under some particular, determinate aspect or another.

2 Aspects and Concepts

It has seemed obvious to many readers of Wittgenstein that what he calls 'aspects' may aptly be identified with, or in terms of, concepts, so that in the formula "perceiving *x* as *y*", "*y*" stands for a *concept*, or is to be understood in terms of one – namely, the *concept* (of) *y*. This idea has sometimes been combined with a second idea that will be discussed in Sections 4 and 5 – namely, that all (normal) perception is aspect perception – to form, or support, the third idea that all (normal adult human) perception is 'conceptualized'.[9] I believe all three ideas are mistaken. Far from lending support to the idea that all perception is conceptualized, aspect perception – by which I mean, aspect dawning – actually provides strong evidence against that idea. But in order to see that, we need to see what is wrong with the first and second ideas. And since there seem to have been – there certainly could, logically, be – those who espouse the first idea but not the second,[10] or the second idea but not the first,[11] I will consider each one of those ideas separately from the other, devoting the present section to the first idea and Sections 4 and 5 to the second idea.[12] In this section, I will argue that the identification of aspects with (or in terms of) concepts is mistaken. More precisely, I will try to show that it is not really clear what the idea is, or what it comes to. My argument may therefore be read as an invitation to those who have proposed to identify aspects with concepts to clarify their proposal.

Wittgenstein himself, as far as I can tell, was not altogether clear on this issue. Though, as I will propose, his grammatical characterization of aspects suggests that, and why, it would be a mistake to identify them with concepts, other remarks encourage that idea. At one point, for example, he proposes that in the dawning of an aspect, 'it is as if one had brought a concept to what one sees, and one now sees the concept along with the thing' (RPPI, 961). I think it matters that Wittgenstein is being quite tentative and metaphorical in this and similar remarks, whereas many of his readers have tended to read such remarks as

---

[9] Three of the most prominent proponents of this combination of ideas have been Strawson, Wollheim, and Fodor; though in Strawson and Wollheim the third idea seems to be reached on more or less independent – in Strawson, broadly Kantian – grounds, and then is taken to receive support from Wittgenstein's remarks on aspect perception. Strawson's and Wollheim's views will be discussed in this and the Section 3. Fodor's view is summarized, 'with permission', by Ned Block thus: '(1) No seeing without seeing as; (2) No seeing as without conceptualization; (3) No conceptualization without concepts' (2014, 561). I will argue in what follows that (1) and (2) are false, at least so long as "seeing-as" means what it means in Wittgenstein. Searle's position vis-à-vis the three ideas is tricky, since he seems to endorse the second and third ideas – claiming (without argument as far as I can tell, and without so much as even an explication of the claim) that 'all seeing is *seeing as* and all seeing is *seeing that*' (Searle 2015, 110) – but does not make clear how the seeing-as is supposed to relate to the seeing-that.

[10] Charles Travis *might* be one. He sometimes seems to espouse the first idea, at least in the case of some aspects (see fn. 18); and he clearly rejects the second (cf. 2013, 102 and 180; and 2015, 45).

[11] Stephen Mulhall *might* be one. He certainly espouses the second idea; and his explication of aspects in terms of Heidegger's notion of "readiness-to-hand" suggests that he would reject the first. In Section 5, however, I will suggest that Mulhall is tacitly relying on the identification of aspects with concepts in his argument for continuous aspect perception.

[12] I have argued against the third idea – that all (normal human adult) perception is conceptualized – as advocated by John McDowell, in Baz (2003). In Baz (2019), I argue against McDowell's more recent version of that idea. All of the basic ingredients of my argument against the third idea may be found in the argument, presented in these pages, against the first two.

literal and non-tentative. And while I think I know what sort of experience Wittgenstein is trying to express in remarks such as this one, and though I myself found such remarks useful for certain purposes in some of my early writings on aspect perception – for example, in emphasizing, as against the idea that aspects may be perceived continuously, the ineliminable role in aspect perception of *attending to the object in a particular way* – they now seem to me problematic. I now believe that it is actually unclear what taking such remarks literally could possibly mean, or come to; and even when taken metaphorically, it is not altogether clear what they are inviting us to imagine, or whether they truly elucidate the seeing of aspects, as opposed to only giving us the illusion of understanding it.

When, under inspiration from Wittgenstein, Strawson suggests that what Wittgenstein calls 'seeing something as something' is a visual experience that 'is irradiated by, or infused with, the concept; or it becomes soaked with the concept' (1982, 93), and Wollheim suggests that 'when I see x as f [where 'f' refers to a concept, AB], f permeates or mixes into the perception' (1980, 219–20), and Agam-Segal proposes that seeing the duck-rabbit as a duck is 'experiencing the concept "duck" impregnating this picture with a particular meaning' (2019, 23), their *language* is certainly metaphorical, but *they* are being neither metaphorical nor tentative: Wittgenstein's "as if" is gone, and the attempt is to give an account of what literally happens whenever we perceive something *as* something. Strawson and Wollheim then go a step further and propose that aspect perception, or seeing-as, thus understood in terms of bringing concepts to what we perceive, characterizes *all* (normal? adult? human?) perception. I will address the idea that all perception is aspect perception, or seeing-as, in Sections 4 and 5. In this section, I am focusing just on the idea that Wittgensteinian aspects may be identified with, or in terms of, concepts. What exactly is the idea? What exactly does it come to? To answer this question, we must first look for what is meant, or could possibly be meant, by "concept" in those accounts.

If we follow Wittgenstein (and Austin), and begin by reminding ourselves how the word "concept" functions in ordinary and normal discourse, I believe we will find that "the concept of x" is often interchangeable with "the meaning of 'x'", and means something like "whatever it is that 'x' carries with it to particular occasions of its use, and makes it fit for some uses but not others".[13] Our everyday criterion for "possessing the concept (of) x", and similarly for "knowing the

---

[13] "Concept" may also mean something like an approach to, or a way of looking at and doing things, as in "The management of the company has come up with an altogether different concept of marketing". But *that* could not possibly be what Strawson, Wollheim, and others who have proposed to identify aspects with concepts mean by "concept", or must mean by it given the story they seem to be trying to tell.

meaning of '*x*'", is the ability to employ "*x*" competently in a wide enough range of contexts, and to respond competently to other people's employment of it. On this understanding of "concept", to possess any one concept is to possess *very many* others and to master a wide and open-ended range of interrelated *practices*. Now, if *that* is how those who propose to identify aspects with concepts understand "concept", then their reasoning might be that since we normally *use words* in expressing the perception of aspects, and since, on this understanding, *every* use of some word "*y*" may be said to be "an application of the concept *y*", then *ipso facto* we are applying concepts in giving voice to the perception of aspects. That understanding of "concept" would purchase the legitimacy of talking about the application of concepts in aspect perception at the price of making it uninformative, empty: one might as well say that we are applying the concept (of) *help* when crying out "Help!" in distress. And it would still be wholly unclear how the *identification* of aspects with concepts is supposed to be understood, how we are supposed to understand Strawson's talk of a perceptual experience that is 'irradiated by, or infused or soaked with, a *concept*',[14] or Wollheim's talk of 'a *concept* permeating, or mixing into the perception', or Agam-Segal's talk of 'the *concept* "duck"' impregnating [the duck-rabbit] picture with a particular meaning', and how that sort of talk is supposed to help us better understand aspect perception, let alone perception more generally. You might as well propose to explain or elucidate the experience someone might naturally express by crying "I feel so lost!", for example, or "I can't take this anymore!", by saying that it is irradiated, or permeated, or impregnated, or . . . by the concept of *being lost*, or *being unable to take it anymore*.

---

[14] Strawson, when trying to enlist Wittgenstein's remarks on aspects in support of his broadly Kantian argument to the effect that all (normal? adult? human?) perception is conceptualized, notes this fundamental difference between how Kant understands "concept" and how Wittgenstein does. 'Wittgenstein's special preoccupations', Strawson writes, 'pull him to the behavioural side of things, to which Kant pays little or no attention' (1982, 94). He then tries to hold on to his earlier, Kantian, story about *concepts* irradiating or soaking perception, even while allowing the Wittgensteinian, 'behavioral' understanding of "concept":

> But we can no more think of the behavioural dispositions as merely externally related to other perceptions than we can think of them as merely externally related to the present perception. Thus the relevant behaviour in reporting an aspect may be to point to other objects of perception. Or in the case of seeing a real, as opposed to a picture-object, as a such-and-such, the behavioural disposition includes, or entails, a readiness for, or expectancy of, other perceptions, of a certain character, of the same object (Strawson 1982, 94).

The understanding of "concept" here is perhaps broad and vague enough so as to make innocuous the talk of *concepts* irradiating or soaking perception: there is no denying that the dawning aspect is *somehow* related to other objects and moments of our experience. The question is how we are to understand that relation. And I still find that the attempt to answer that question in terms of *concepts* is, at best, uninformative, and, at worst, seriously misleading, in encouraging an overly-intellectualized picture of our pre-reflective perceptual experience. I'll come back to this in Sections 4 and 5.

It is fairly clear, however, that those who have sought to identify aspects with concepts have been relying on a narrower, representationalist understanding of "concept" that is common in philosophy, linguistics, and psychology. On that understanding, "the concept of f" is supposed to refer to whatever ultimately guides us in 'categorizing', or 'classifying', things in the world as "f" or "not-f" (or neither clearly "f" nor clearly "not-f"), and where that categorization or classification is taken to be more or less independent of whatever *else* we do with "f", and of our linguistic practices more broadly. Concepts, thus understood, are elements of Kantian "cognitions", or Fregean "thoughts", and are paradigmatically applied in objective, true-or-false judgments.[15] Elsewhere I have argued, following Wittgenstein, that when it comes to philosophically troublesome words such as "know", "cause", or "intention", the representationalist conception has led philosophers astray.[16] But since there is no denying that *some* of what we do with words is represent things truly or falsely – though still *not* practice-independently – and since Wittgenstein himself seems to allow that the representationalist conception *might* be philosophically harmless when it comes to words such as "table", "chair", and "bread" (PI, 1), and therefore I suppose also to words such as "duck" and "rabbit", let's see if this narrower understanding of "concept" could help us make sense of, and make plausible, the identification of aspects with concepts.

The first thing I wish to note is that with some aspects that dawn on us, no description – no particular "y" – and therefore no candidate concept, readily suggests itself. One may all of a sudden be struck by the expression of a face, or by the atmosphere in a party (or *something* about it), or by someone's peculiar way of walking into a room, and find it hard, or even impossible, to put it satisfyingly into words. And even if one does manage to come up with a description of what has struck one – saying of a drawn face, for example, or of its expression, that 'it looks like a complacent businessman, stupidly supercilious, who though fat, imagines he is a lady killer' (Wittgenstein 1958, 162) – one may still only '[mean this] as an *approximate* description of the expression' (Wittgenstein 1958, 162, my emphasis), and perhaps also say something like 'words can't exactly describe it' (Wittgenstein 1958, 162). In such cases, the aspect that strikes us, or dawns on us, is what Kant calls 'an aesthetic idea': '[a] presentation of the imagination that compels (*veranlasst*) much thinking, but to which no determinate thought whatsoever, i.e. no *concept*, can be adequate'

---

[15] Here is Paul Bloom, articulating the prevailing way of thinking about concepts, in philosophy as well as in psychology: '[G]rasp of the conditions underlying category membership is usually described as a concept, and the concept that is associated with a word is usually described as the word's meaning' (Bloom 2000, 145).

[16] Baz (2012 and 2017a).

(Kant 2000, 314, Kant's emphasis). Such aspects are not uncommon – though they may easily be overlooked if one takes the ambiguous figures as one's paradigmatic examples of aspect perception – and I don't suppose anyone would propose to identify them with concepts. Insofar as we use language to express and try to share our experience of them, its use is precisely that: to try to get others to share, and thereby validate, our experience of the thing, not to capture that thing as it is independently of our, or anyone's experience of it, as the application of concepts normally aims to do.

Let's consider next an example of an aspect for which a particular description does immediately suggest itself: Wittgenstein's example of being struck by the likeness of a face we are looking at to another. Even though a particular description of the aspect does readily suggest itself here – i.e. "a similarity to so and so, or to so and so's face" – it is still none too clear what the candidate *concept* might be in this case. No obvious *generality* suggests itself under which the face we're looking at might have been subsumed, or for that matter perceived, when its similarity to another struck us; there is only *this* one face, and *that* other one. We see *the other face* in *this* one. This points toward an understanding, which will be proposed in Section 3, of the aspect's particular (non-conceptual) way of transcending the object in which it is perceived, and connecting it with others.

If we were committed to the idea that aspects are to be identified with, or in terms of, concepts, however, and therefore committed to finding some such concept in the case of the dawning similarity of one face to another, I suppose the most plausible candidate would be the empirical concept of *bearing (some) visible similarity to a particular, given face*. Being a concept, it is, as already noted, *general*: it allows for indefinitely many instantiations that differ from each other in any number of ways; and it transcends any finite set of instantiations: for any particular face, and for any finite set of faces that may all correctly be judged to bear visible similarity to that face, there could always be another face that is visibly distinguishable from all of those faces and yet may correctly be judged to bear visible similarity to the first face. One could go a step further and argue that *any* two faces may, in *some* contexts, correctly be judged to bear *some* visible similarity to each other.

This leads us to the further point that, as Charles Travis has taught us to recognize, the concept *bearing visible similarity to a particular face*, just like any other empirical concept, is 'context-sensitive': for any given face, and for a wide variety of faces that *in some contexts* would correctly count as bearing visible similarity to it, there could be other contexts in which those same faces would not correctly count as bearing visible similarity to that face. This means that in judging that one face bears (or does not bear) visible similarity to another, we are beholden, not just to the two faces, but also to the context in which we make the judgment. And if someone were to ask us, apart from a context suitable for fixing what "bear visible similarity" means (in that context), whether two given faces bear visible similarity to each other, the correct response would, in most cases, be "yes, or no, depending on what you mean, on how your words are (to be) understood".

I think these reminders should already give pause to anyone who wishes to claim that what blends with (mixes into, infuses, impregnates . . .) our perception of a face, when its likeness to another face strikes us, is a *concept*; not because they show that the claim might be mistaken, but because they suggest that it is not even clear what exactly is being claimed. And they furthermore raise the suspicion that the identification of aspects with concepts rests for its apparent sense, and plausibility, on a conflation of the *concept* of *y* with something like an *image* or *perceptual schema* of *y*, or perhaps various experiences or bodily responses or attitudes that have become associated for us with "*y*".[17] – But let's move closer.

Concepts, as commonly thought of in Western philosophy at least since Kant, and in contemporary analytic philosophy, are paradigmatically applied to the world in objective, truth evaluable *judgments*. As noted in Section 1, however, it is important that the case Wittgenstein describes is *not* one of judging that the one face *is* similar to the other.[18] In fact, it seems clear that, in the normal case at least, what we perceive something *as* is something we are *not* taking it, let alone claiming it, *to be*. Nor are we *imagining* that something *being* that other thing. In some cases of aspect perception, it is not even clear what it would mean for us to try to.[19]

---

[17] Travis, and precisely because he is clearer than others on what he means by "concept" and careful not to make any such conflation, runs into more obvious difficulties when he tries to accommodate Wittgensteinian aspects within his Fregean dichotomy between concepts and their instances. I discuss those difficulties, and argue that the Wittgensteinian aspect fits on neither side of that dichotomy, in Baz (2019).

[18] Travis, who attempts to account for the perception of Wittgensteinian aspects from within the Fregean dichotomy between the objective and the metaphysically private, proposes that some aspects – among them the similarity between two faces – are objective. 'If you see a resemblance between a man's face and his father's, you see, so far, something there to be seen', he writes, and 'You would be disappointed to learn this was not so' (2015, 53). But if a resemblance between a person's face and his father's has struck me – where this is the perceptual *experience* Wittgenstein describes at PPF, 114, in which I come to see the father's face in the face I'm looking at, so that the perceived physiognomy of the face I'm looking at changes, and changes wholly, rather than the perceptual *judgment* that there *is* an objectively establishable similarity between the two faces – then I do not know what it would mean "to learn this was not so".

[19] Wollheim's claim that 'we cannot see something as something it (or its counterpart) could never have been' (1980, 222) seems to fly directly in the face, not only of some of Wittgenstein's examples – in what sense could the letter F have *been* facing right, or left? – but also of some of Wollheim's own examples. How is this claim supposed to be true of the case of seeing a church as

The empirical judgment that something is (an) *f*, and so if you will the subsumption of a case under the empirical concept *f*, situates the object and its property of being *f* in the objective world – within what Charles Travis calls 'networks of factive meaning' (cf. Travis 2013, 91). A particular face's *being* similar to some other particular face, for example, factively means certain objectively establishable things (and indicates or makes likely certain other things), where 'factively' here means: if those other things do not hold, then either the similarity of the one face to the other does not mean them or the similarity does not hold. Because empirical judgments, and more broadly Kantian "cognitions" *(Erkenntnisse)*, are interconnected and form a system – the system Kant calls 'nature' (cf. Kant 1998, A216/B263) – they commit those who make any one judgment to indefinitely many other Kantian cognitions, or Fregean thoughts. They also commit them *practically*. Empirical concepts, understood as constituents of empirical judgments (or cognitions), or as what those judgments apply to cases, may accordingly be thought of as individuated or defined by those commitments, regardless of whether particular *applications* of them are committed or somehow uncommitted (hypothetical, counterfactual).[20] If I *judge* that one face *is* visibly similar to another, for example, then I am committed to expecting all normal and competent people who are suitably positioned to recognize this; and I am committed to holding those who deny the similarity to be mistaken, and to be liable to err practically as a result; and I am committed to taking it that each of the two faces, or some feature(s) of it, may be pointed to as a way of giving someone (some) information about the other face ("The escaped suspect's face (nose) is similar to so and so's face (nose)"); and I'm committed to there being certain objectively establishable features of the faces that are responsible for the similarity, so that if *those* features were sufficiently altered in one of the faces, the similarity – I mean, *that* similarity – would cease to exist; and I am committed to being able to identify those features – to specify in what the similarity consists ("They have the same pointy and slightly crooked nose"); and so on and so forth.[21] If I am not thus committed, I have not thus judged.

---

an overturned footstool (1980, 222), or a mountain range as a naked woman's body (1980, 222)? If any sense could be given to the claim that a church (or its counterpart) could have been an overturned footstool or that a mountain range (or its counterpart) could have been a naked woman's body, then, in *that* sense, anything could have been anything else, and the condition is empty.

[20] This connects with Kant's saying that the modality of a judgment 'contributes nothing to the content of the judgment' (1998, A74/B100).

[21] This list of commitments is not meant to be complete; and it does not even matter whether it is accurate (as far as it goes). What matters for my purposes is that an accurate (even if still incomplete) list of this sort *may* be given.

It is true that when I merely *imagine* that – or imagine a state of affairs in which – one face bears a visible similarity to another, I do not commit myself as I do when I *judge* that it does. But *what* I imagine may still be defined or specified in terms of the same set of commitments:[22] what I imagine is, precisely, a state of affairs in which there is an empirically establishable visible similarity between the faces, where *that* means a situation in which the two faces are such that normal and competent perceivers who are suitably positioned may rightfully be expected to find them similar to each other (given a suitable context); and in which those who denied the similarity would be mistaken and would be liable to err practically as a result; and in which each of the two faces, or some feature(s) of it, would be such that it could be pointed to as a way of giving someone some information about the other face; and in which the faces have certain objectively establishable features – identifiable by normal and competent perceivers who are suitably positioned – that make them similar to each other; and so on and so forth.

A Wittgensteinian aspect, by contrast – and this goes for such aspects as the duck- or rabbit-aspect of the duck-rabbit, or the two aspects of the Necker cube, no less than for the similarity between the faces – is not similarly situated within a network of factive meanings; it is not a feature of the objective world. While *my being struck* by the similarity between two faces *is* an objectively establishable fact, and as such means, factively, any number of objectively establishable things (mostly things about *me*), the *similarity between the faces* that strikes me – and the same goes for the duck- or rabbit-aspect, the two aspects of the Necker, and so on – though it may affect me in any number of more or less significant ways, does not (factively) mean, or indicate, or make likely, *anything* objectively establishable. *It* is not part of the objective ('external') world. Nor is it imagined to be part of the objective world. But if so, I'm proposing, then it may not aptly be identified in terms of the empirical concept of *bearing visible similarity*.

And yet, for all that, the aspect – in the case under consideration, the similarity that has dawned on me of one face to another – is not merely subjective. Both phenomenologically and grammatically, it is *there*, in the perceived face. Though I cannot objectively establish its presence, or describe it geometrically, or prove wrong those who fail to see it, I still take it that others could be brought to see it there too, and I take it that they are missing something *about the face* if they don't.[23] Though the (Kantian, objective) 'I think' could

---

[22] This is really just the basic Fregean truth, emphasized by Geach (1965), that (what may count as) the *same* thought may, on the one hand, be *asserted* or otherwise committed to and, on the other hand, be merely "entertained" or "considered" (or imagined to be true).

[23] This, I argue in Baz (2019), means that the aspect fits on neither side of Travis's guiding dichotomy between 'objects in the environment' and Fregean '*Vorstellungen*'. One of Travis's central contentions is that only the former are proper objects of perception, and that failure to acknowledge this would lead us straightaway to positing objects of the second kind as objects of

not sensibly attach to our experience of the aspect, neither the experience nor the aspect are 'nothing to us' (contra Kant 1998, B131).

A long tradition, beginning with Kant's *Critique of Pure Reason* (at least on one popular reading of it) and exerting its strong influence all the way to the present, would have us suppose that only the subsumption of what presents itself to us in our experience under *concepts* – thought of as systematically interrelated rules for the unification and organization of the 'sensible manifold' – could enable us to move from the merely "inner" or "subjective" succession of *Vorstellungen* to a world sharable with others (see Kant 1998, A196-7/B242).[24] Part of what Wittgenstein has taught us to recognize, or reminded us, is that what may sensibly be called "the application of concepts" could itself only truly be understood in terms of inter-subjectively shared practices into which we are initiated, and in which we participate, in, and against the background of, a cultural-historical world – Wittgenstein's 'form of life' – that is, to some degree, *always already* shared with others.[25] This is a point of deep agreement between Wittgenstein and phenomenologists such as Heidegger and, especially, Merleau-Ponty. But as those phenomenologists have taught us to recognize, it is inherently difficult to describe without distortion our perceptual relation to the not-yet-objective but nonetheless intersubjectively sharable world. In particular, it is extremely difficult to resist the temptation to objectify the world *as perceived* and *responded to* prior to being *thought* (or *talked*) *about*, and to think of our relation to it in terms of the very same empirical concepts whose application may only be understood, if Wittgenstein and the phenomenologists are correct, against the background of that very relation. This, I will propose in Section 6, is a place where the dawning of Wittgensteinian aspects could prove philosophically enlightening, and precisely because it brings out a perceptual relation to the world that is not yet 'mediated by concepts'.[26]

3 Aspects as Perceived Internal Relations

I have argued in Section 2 that Wittgensteinian aspects may not aptly be identified with concepts. It is, however, undeniable that the aspect does,

perception and the bases of perceptual judgments (cf. Travis 2013, 183), which he takes – correctly in my view – to be hopeless (cf. Travis 2013, 193 and 387). In arguing for this, Travis repeatedly reminds us of the grammatical truth that 'what someone saw is bounded by what there was, anyway, to be seen' (Travis 2013, 411; see also 102), so that 'if Penelope is not sipping [a mojito], Sid does not see [her sipping a mojito]' (Travis 2013, 266); and that seems to me just right, but only as long as we are talking about the grammar of "see" in what Wittgenstein refers to as its 'first use' – a use that Wittgenstein contrasts with the use of that word in which it refers to the seeing of aspects (PPF, 111).

[24] Similar ideas may be found in Frege (cf. Frege 1956, 306 and 309).
[25] I argue for this understanding of Wittgenstein's 'form of life' in Baz (2018).
[26] Wollheim 1980, 219.

somehow, connect the thing we are perceiving under it with other things in our world – *this* face with *that* face, *this* ambiguous drawing with *ducks* or *rabbits* (drawn or flesh and blood), the Necker cube with *things oriented this or that way relative to us*, and so on. How are we to understand the aspect's way of transcending the particular thing and connecting it with others, if not in terms of a concept or generality under which the thing is subsumed (however hypothetically or imaginatively)?

'What I perceive in the dawning of an aspect', Wittgenstein writes, 'is not a property of the object, but an internal relation between it and other objects' (PPF, 247). Though the notion of "internal relation" features already in the *Tractatus*, where it is used to say something – however ultimately discoverable as 'nonsensical' – about '[the relation of] depicting that holds between language and the world' (Wittgenstein 2001, 4.014),[27] I wish to propose that the notion, as Wittgenstein uses it *here*, is drawn from Gestalt psychology and is, importantly, a *perceptual* notion, as opposed to an objective, third-personal notion.[28] Having said that, and though we will shortly see further evidence supporting the attribution to the later Wittgenstein of the understanding of "internal relation" I'm about to elaborate, what matters for my present purposes is not whether my proposed interpretation of PPF, 247 succeeds in capturing what Wittgenstein had in mind when he wrote it, but rather whether it provides a compelling answer to the question with which I opened this section.

Two (or more) perceived things (objects, elements) stand in an internal relation to each other when their perceived qualities are not independent of the perceived relation between them, or, in other words, when how each one of them perceptually presents itself affects how the other perceptually presents itself. Here is a passage from Kurt Koffka that illustrates the notion of "internal relation" as I'm proposing it should be understood in connection with aspect-perception: 'Two colors adjacent to each other are not perceived as two independent things, but as having an inner connection which is at the same time a factor determining the special qualities A and B themselves' (1927, 221). According to Gestalt psychology, what we perceive, at the most basic level, is not atomic sensations or localized qualities that we must then somehow synthesize into significant, intelligible wholes, but rather unified, significant wholes, where the perceived qualities of the elements of a perceived whole – and so the

[27] For an illuminating discussion of the different ways – 'metaphysical' and 'anti-metaphysical' – of understanding "internal relation" as used in the *Tractatus*, see McGinn (2010).

[28] Schroeder muddles his discussion of aspect perception, it seems to me, by speaking of the similarity that strikes us as at once 'an internal relation' (2010, 359) and 'an objective feature of the object, namely a relation of likeness between it and some other object' (2010, 360). But how is an objective similarity of one object to another an *internal* relation between the two objects?

specific contributions those elements make to the overall perceived significance, or gestalt, of that whole – are not perceptually independent of its
perceived overall significance.

The duck-rabbit provides a simple – even if also importantly simplistic –
illustration of this. When you see it as a rabbit, say, you see the two appendages
as ears; but your seeing them as ears is not independent of your seeing the whole
thing as a rabbit. Perceptually, the ears are (seen as) ears only when the whole
thing is (seen as) a rabbit. One important thing this means is that your seeing the
duck-rabbit as a rabbit cannot be *explained*, or *rationalized*, as the outcome of
your seeing this portion of the drawing as ears, that portion as mouth, another
portion as the back of the head, and so on. The rabbit aspect is not synthesized
from elements that have their "rabbit-parts" significance independently of being
elements of that overall aspect. On the other hand, if you took the basic elements
of our perception of the duck-rabbit to only have objectively establishable,
geometrical properties, and so to be devoid of any rabbit (and equally duck)
significance, then you would never be able to explain, just on *that* basis, why
those elements got synthesized into the rabbit aspect, say, rather than the duck
aspect. This shows that the perception of significant wholes should be taken as
phenomenologically primary. And that, I'm about to propose, is true not only
when the whole in question is some individual object taken in (artificial)
isolation, but also when it includes some such object and the perceptual
background against which it is perceived in the natural course of everyday
experience.[29]

Wittgenstein gives clear, if also characteristically non-theoretical, expression
to this fundamental feature of human perception – and at the same time provides
further evidence for the attribution to him of the understanding I have just
offered of "internal relation" – in the following remark:

> Look at a long familiar piece of furniture in its old place in your room. You
> would like to say: "It is part of an organism". Or "Take it outside, and it is no
> longer at all the same as it was", and similar things. And naturally one isn't
> thinking of any *causal* dependence of one part on the rest. Rather it is like
> this: ... [I]f I tried taking it *quite* out of its present context, I should say that it
> had ceased to exist and another had got into its place.

---

[29] That the analysis of perceptual experience presupposes its synthesis and therefore cannot explain
it, is one of Kant's fundamental insights and his most basic objection to empiricist-mechanistic
accounts of how unity arises in our experience. Kant saw that we must play an active role in
bringing about, or constituting, the unity of our experience. What Kant missed in the *Critique of
Pure Reason*, Merleau-Ponty suggests, and later arguably came to recognize when thinking
about the experience of beauty, is the possibility of a synthesis that, while in some clear sense
intelligible and intersubjectively shareable, is not (aptly thought of as) conceptual(ized) (see PP,
xvii/lxxxi).

One might even feel like this: "Everything is part and parcel of everything else" (*external and internal relations* [my emphasis, AB]). Displace a piece and it is no longer what it was [. . .] (RPPI, 339).

In the Appendix, I will propose that Wittgenstein's tentative tone, in this remark and in other remarks in which he is moved to describe our perceptual experience, is due, at least in part, to a misplaced mistrust of phenomenology. For Merleau-Ponty and Gestalt psychologists, what Wittgenstein says here is just right *when said about the phenomenal world*: how anything we attend to presents itself to us perceptually is internally related to the background against which it is perceived; and that goes not only for its more or less geographically immediate background, but for anything that contributes, however remotely and indeterminately, to its perceived significance.[30]

Another case of gestalt perception, which is at the heart of Wittgenstein's understanding of philosophical difficulty, is that of *linguistically*-expressed meaning, or sense. (From Merleau-Ponty's perspective, the gestalt-like nature of linguistic sense is but a special case of what is true of all perceived sense, whether linguistically-expressed or not.) On Wittgenstein's view, which may be seen as a development of Frege's 'context principle' (1999, x), the basic unit of linguistic sense is neither the isolated word, nor the isolated string of words, but an utterance – a human *act* performed against the background of the history of the language, the culture, and of the individual participants (cf. PI 19, 49, 117, and 199). 'The total speech act in the total speech situation', as Austin puts it (1999, 147). Phenomenologically – which means, from the perspective we all occupy as speakers engaged in discourse (as opposed to theoreticians reflecting on it) – the analysis of linguistic sense presupposes its synthesis: the contribution made by each word to the overall sense of an utterance is not independent of, and therefore cannot analytically *explain*, or *rationalize*, that overall sense.[31] It is only when, or to the extent that, you see the overall sense of an utterance, that you can see what contribution each of the words is making that that overall sense.

Internal relations, I've suggested, hold not just among the perceived elements of perceived objects but also, and equally fundamentally, between perceived

---

[30] In *The Visible and the Invisible*, and partly under the inspiration of Saussure, Merleau-Ponty goes as far as to suggest that a perceived red dress is a 'punctuation in the field of red things, which includes the tiles of roof tops, the flags of gatekeepers and of the revolution, certain terrains near Aix or in Madagascar, it is also a punctuation in the field of red garments, which includes, along with the dresses of woman, robes of Professors, bishops, and advocate generals, and also in the field of adornments and of uniforms' (1968, 132).

[31] On this, Wittgenstein and Merleau-Ponty are in full agreement. 'In understanding others', Merleau-Ponty writes, 'the problem is always indeterminate; because only the solution to the problem will make the givens retrospectively appear as convergent . . . ' (PP, 179/184; see also 389/408–9). I develop this important affinity between Wittgenstein and Merleau-Ponty in some detail, in chapter 5 of Baz (2017a).

objects and the background against which they are perceived. This is illustrated in Wittgenstein's example of the old piece of furniture that 'ceases to exist' – perceptually, experientially – when taken out of its familiar context, and may be seen as well in the perception of linguistic sense. 'To understand a sentence', Wittgenstein writes, 'is to understand a language' (PI 199); and 'to imagine a language means to imagine a form of life' (PI, 19).

The internal relation between figure and background is likely to be missed in the case of aspect-perception, however, if we mostly focus on the schematic drawings and figures that were designed to be ambiguous. These objects are typically encountered in the artificial context of a psychology lab or philosophy classroom. They are therefore 'cut off', as Merleau-Ponty puts it, from our perceptual field, with its temporally structured and extended personal and cultural 'horizons'; and it is precisely that artificial insulation of those objects that makes it possible for us to project different perceptual physiognomies on them, more or less at will (PP, 279–80/292). Even here, the perceived objects stand in internal relations to other objects, as Wittgenstein suggests in PPF, 247; but the way in which foreground and background are internally related in normal perception, and therefore change together, does not come out clearly in the case of such artificially isolated objects. It comes out far more clearly in the more natural cases of aspect dawning.

Consider the experience Wittgenstein describes of being struck by the similarity between two faces. A similarity understood as an objective property of the faces is an *external* relation between them: each face has its objectively establishable properties, which one may come to know without knowing anything about the other face; and those properties determine whether, and if so to what extent, the two may correctly count (context-dependently) as bearing some objective similarity to each other. And so you may look at a face and see (in Wittgenstein's first sense of "see"), or have someone point out or demonstrate to you, that there is some visible similarity between it and another, where seeing *that* need not involve, or bring about, *any* change in how you visually experience the face you're looking at: its perceived gestalt (physiognomy, expression) need not change at all.

By contrast, in the experience Wittgenstein describes, the perceived gestalt of the face you're looking at changes; and what dawns on you here is an *internal* relation between the one face and the other, precisely because the perceived relation – here, of similarity – is inseparable from the perceived change in the overall physiognomy or expression of the face. The perceived qualities of each of the two faces that make them bear a similarity to each other are not independent, perceptually, from our perception of the similarity. (Again, they *could be*: we could recognize an objectively establishable similarity between the faces – a similarity that may simply be *known* to be there, and which does not depend on anyone's visual experience of the faces. But that would not be the seeing of a Wittgensteinian aspect – the *seeing* of one thing *as* another. As Wittgenstein notes, even the person he calls 'aspect-blind' and defines as someone 'lacking in the capacity to see something *as something*' should be able to recognize objective similarity and 'execute such orders as "Bring me something that looks like *this*"' (PPF, 257)!)

The perceived, dawning similarity of one face to another, I've proposed, is an internal relation between the two faces – a way of bringing *individual things* together perceptually without (yet, or necessarily) subsuming them both under some concept, or generality that, as such, transcends them and any other finite set of its instances. What the two faces share is a perceived, experienced, physiognomy – which may often be quite indeterminate and hard to put satisfyingly into words – not a determinate, empirical concept of which they may both be judged to be instances.

The same is true when, in trying to get another person to hear a musical theme in a particular way, one says, 'Here it is as though a conclusion were being drawn, here as though someone were expressing an agreement, or as though *this* were a reply to what came before' (Wittgenstein 1980c, 52). Our understanding of such invitations to hear one thing as another presupposes, as Wittgenstein notes, 'familiarity with *conclusions, expressions of agreement, replies*' (Wittgenstein 1980c, 52, my emphasis). Once again, the invitation is to perceive – effect perceptually for oneself – an internal relation between one thing (here, the theme, or a part of it) and other moments or elements of one's experience (here, of human discourse). In this way, 'the theme interacts with language': 'the rhythm of our language, of our thinking and feeling' is the background against which the theme acquires its perceived sense for us, becomes understandable in some particular way (Wittgenstein 1980c, 52); and, at the same time, the theme itself becomes 'a new part of our language [. . .] becomes incorporated into it [. . .] we learn a new *gesture*' (Wittgenstein 1980c, 52). In a similar way, 'a whole world of pain [may be] contained' in, or 'bound up with', the words 'Fare well!' (Wittgenstein 1980c, 52). And to insist that what we hear in the words when we hear a whole world of pain contained in them is a *concept* – and which concept might that be? of pain? of a whole world of pain? – would distort the perceptual experience it purports to elucidate, or else distort our concept of concept.

This, I wish to propose, is how we should think about other Wittgensteinian aspects as well: seeing the duck-rabbit as a duck, or as a rabbit; seeing the letter F as facing right, or left, seeing the Necker cube as going *this* way, or *that* . . . In all of those cases, I'm proposing, the aspect is a perceived, experienced physiognomy that connects it internally – not necessarily by way of *similarity!*[32] – with other elements of the phenomenal world. That physiognomy may of course be described, more or less satisfyingly; and, in some cases, its (first) description would be readily available ("duck", for example, or "reply to what came before"). But to describe an object's perceived physiognomy, or the aspect under which it is perceived, I have been arguing, is not the same as applying to it an empirical concept, or subsuming it under one – not under any common or plausible understanding of the latter, at any rate.[33]

4 *Continuous* Aspect Perception?

It has seemed obvious to some readers of Wittgenstein's remarks on aspects that what he calls "aspect perception" has a continuous form, and that the experience of aspect-dawning should be understood against the background of that continuous perceptual relation to things that may aptly be called "continuous aspect perception". For readers such as Strawson and Wollheim, who have on more or less independent grounds come to espouse the idea that all (normal, adult, human) perception is, or must be, conceptualized, and for whom aspect perception as discussed by Wittgenstein seemed to give us purchase over that idea, the reality of

---

[32] That the internal relations among elements of our perceptual field need not be ones of similarity should already be clear even just from the case of the duck-rabbit: the different elements of the rabbit-aspect, for example, are internally related to each other, but are not perceptually similar to each other. Normally, the immediate background against which we perceive something as we do, and which is internally related to it in the way, or sense, I've described, is not similar to it, or composed (exclusively) of elements that are. This is clearly expressed by Merleau-Ponty, when he writes about the red color of a particular dress: '[T]his red is what it is only by connecting up from its place with other reds about it, with which it forms a constellation, *or with other colors it dominates or that dominate it, that it attracts or that attract it, that it repels or that repel it*' (1968, 132, my emphasis). A nice illustration of an experienced internal relation that is not one of similarity may be found in Alice Munro's story, 'The Beggar Maid'. Rose, who comes from a poor background, is awarded a fellowship to go to college, and finds accommodation in the middle-class house of Dr. Henshawe. And what she finds is that Dr. Henshawe's house destroys for her 'the naturalness, the taken-for-granted background' of the house she grew up in. What the two houses do best, Rose finds, is 'discredit each other' (Munro 1996, 153–4). Perceptually, experientially, the two houses are internally related: each affects Rose's perception, or experience, of the other; each forms part of the background against which the other acquires its particular perceived significance, or physiognomy, for Rose.

[33] This is not to deny that the ability to see different things as belonging together, or as not belonging together, is essential to the acquisition and application of concepts. In the *Phenomenology of Perception*, Merleau-Ponty argues, on the basis of empirical evidence, that people who have a hard time *seeing* certain things as belonging together, or as "standing out" from the rest, are significantly impaired in their acquisition and use of the most basic common nouns, or categories. 'The categorial activity', he writes, 'before being a thought or a form of knowledge, is a certain manner of relating oneself to the world and, accordingly, a style or shape of experience' (PP, 191/197). That means that the level of perception that aspect-dawning brings out is essential to the acquisition and application of concepts, which is importantly different from – indeed, the reverse of – the common idea argued against in section 2 that the latter explains the former, or is somehow key to understanding it.

continuous aspect perception more or less followed unquestioned: if our perception is always conceptualized, at least normally, and if for perception to be conceptualized just means that anything and everything we perceive – whenever and for however long we perceive it – is perceived *as* this or that, it follows that perceiving-as, and so aspect perception, has a continuous version. For readers such as Mulhall and Johnston, on the other hand, the motivating thought seems to have been that the *dawning* of an aspect may only aptly be understood as a *switch* from one perceptual relation to the thing to another *within a broader category of perceptual relation to things* that may aptly be called "continuous aspect perception". For both parties, the aspect that dawns replaces some other aspect that had been perceived continuously right up until that moment of dawning.

For those like Strawson, who have drawn inspiration and support from Wittgenstein's remarks on aspects for a view of perception that they anyway found compelling, the fact that Wittgenstein himself focuses almost exclusively on the *dawning* or *noticing* of aspects in his remarks was merely an unfortunate 'over-emphasis' on his part (Strawson 1982, 93). For those like Mulhall and Johnston, on the other hand, who were primarily interested in getting Wittgenstein right, as opposed to just drawing on him, his nearly exclusive focus on aspect-dawning was something that needed to be interpreted away. 'Contrary to appearances', Mulhall writes, 'Wittgenstein's primary concern [...] is not the concept of aspect-dawning but rather that of continuous aspect perception [...] [T]he capacity to experience aspect-dawning is of importance primarily because it manifests the general attitude or relation to symbols and people which the concept of continuous aspect perception picks out (1990, 123).[34] 'The importance of

---

[34] One complication that I'm not going to go into in this book is that, as Mulhall's talk here of 'symbols and people' indicates, his proposed account of aspect perception is only fit to apply to cases in which some sort of *representational* relation is supposed to hold – between pictures or drawings and the objects depicted in them, between people's (or other creatures') behavior and the states of mind it expresses, and between words (taken as mere sounds or written symbols) and their meanings or what they express. (I should note that I find thinking of the latter two (behavior and words) on the model of the first (representational pictures and drawings) problematic; but that's a whole other issue.) Mulhall proposes that his account may apply more broadly (see 1990, 137; and 2001, 265); but it is hard to see how it is supposed to do so, precisely because the account – and especially the way it is supposed to 'dissolve' the apparent 'paradox' of aspect-dawning – relies on the presence of some sort of representational relation between one thing and another (cf. Mulhall 2001, 253–4). Johnston, by contrast, readily acknowledges that his proposed account – which is very similar to Mulhall's – only applies to aspect perception in pictures and drawings, human behavior, and words; and he criticizes Mulhall for failing to recognize that (see Johnston 1993, 244). But then, what about all of the aspects that are perceived where no relation of representation between one thing and another is present, as in the case of the dawning similarity of one face to another? And if a relation of representation between one thing and another is not necessary for aspect perception, as those other cases make clear, why suppose it is essential to it even in those cases where some such relation is arguably present? In Baz (2000), I argue that it is not.

aspect-dawning', Johnston agrees, 'is that it draws attention to the wider phenomenon of continuous aspect perception' (1993, 43). But if *that* is why Wittgenstein was so interested in the dawning of aspects, why doesn't he ever just say it? And what about all of his remarks in which he seems to be questioning, and in more than one way, the very intelligibility of the idea of continuous aspect perception?[35]

My plan for this section is as follows. First, I will look at the one place in section xi of part II of the *Investigations* where Wittgenstein talks about the 'continuous (constant, steady, stable, *stegig*) seeing' of an aspect, and will argue that it does not support the idea that something called 'continuous aspect perception' is Wittgenstein's true interest in his remarks on aspects. Having done that, I will consider the several ways in which Wittgenstein explicitly questions the very idea of continuous aspect perception. And then, in Section 5, I will argue that the idea of continuous aspect perception is not only grammatically suspect, but phenomenologically problematic as well. The basic point will be that what Wittgenstein calls '*aspect* perception' requires *taking hold of the object perceptually, attending to it* in a particular way; and that is something that we cannot do continuously, at least not normally. We have only limited control over what we attend to perceptually and how, and our perceptual attention is naturally shifting. In order for the aspect to become continuous it would need to become, precisely, independent of our, or anyone's, perceptually attending to the object, by becoming a piece of (presumed, possible) objective knowledge, or the object of an empirical judgment (however hypothetically or uncommittedly entertained) – and so, if you will, conceptualized. In other words, for the aspect to become continuous it would need to become an object of sight of Wittgenstein's *first* category. And then it would no longer be (what Wittgenstein would call) an *aspect*.

---

[35] Strawson's way of dealing with Wittgenstein's saying that it makes no sense to say of someone that they see something *as* what they know it to *be* – a knife and fork as a knife and fork (PPF, 122–3), for example, or a conventional picture of a lion *as* a lion (PPF, 203) – was to insist, à la Grice's (1989) and Searle's (1999) distinction between what it makes sense to *say* and what would be *true* to say, that while '[n]o doubt it is only against the background of some [...] experience of change of aspects, or of the thought of its possibility, that it is quite natural and non-misleading to speak, in connection with ordinary perception, of seeing objects as the objects they are, [...] this does not make it incorrect or false to do so generally' (1982, 93). Mulhall's way of handling those remarks of Wittgenstein's has been to insist that Wittgenstein is only concerned with aspect-*dawning* in those remarks, and is 'simply denying the ubiquity of experiences of aspect-dawning; [with] no bearing on the ubiquity of continuous aspect perception' (2001, 265). But the problem with the idea of continuous aspect perception is not merely that it makes no sense *to say* of someone that she sees something as what she knows it to be. The problem, as we will see in this section and in Section 5, is that it is not clear what anyone might mean in saying that – what the idea of continuous aspect perception is supposed to come to, exactly – and that extant attempts to cash out that idea, Strawson's and Mulhall's included, have all run, not only against Wittgenstein's grammatical reminders, but also against the phenomenology of perception.

But let's begin with the one place in section xi of Part II of the *Investigations* in which Wittgenstein talks about the 'continuous seeing' of an aspect. After introducing the duck-rabbit, Wittgenstein says:

> And I must distinguish between the 'continuous seeing [*stetigen Sehen*]' of an aspect and the 'lighting up [dawning, *Aufleuchten*]' of an aspect. The picture might have been shown me, and I never have seen anything but a rabbit in it [. . .] (PPF, 118).[36]

> I may, then, have seen the duck-rabbit simply as a picture-rabbit from the first. That is to say, if asked 'What's that?' or 'What do you see here?' I should have replied: 'A picture-rabbit'. If I had further been asked what that was, I would have explained by pointing to all sorts of pictures of rabbits, would perhaps have pointed to real rabbits, talked about their animal life, or given an imitation of them (PPF, 120, translation amended).

> [. . .] I should simply have described my perception: just as if I had said 'I see a red circle over there' (PPF, 121).

The case Wittgenstein here describes is different, both grammatically and phenomenologically, from what he calls 'aspect seeing' or 'aspect perception' almost anywhere else. On my reading of Wittgenstein, he is here setting this sort of case aside to prevent confusion with the sorts of cases, and concepts, he is focusing on, not to signal his true interest in his investigation of aspects. There is no textual support, as far as I can see, for attributing to him the latter intention.

The criterion for someone's "continuously seeing an aspect", as Wittgenstein here describes it, is simply a report of perception, a description – given under fairly special circumstance, as I will shortly note – of what you (take yourself to) know to lie in front of you. A straightforward answer to the question "what's that?" might very well (be used in order to) teach another person something about the external world. The same kind of answer may be given in response to a similarly worded question asked about a non-ambiguous picture – of a red circle, for example – and it would then make no sense to say that the responder is

---

[36] In the next remark, PPF, 119, which I omit, Wittgenstein introduces 'the concept of a picture-object', and notes how, in some respects, we respond to or engage with such picture-objects as we respond to or engage with "real", non-depicted objects. For Mulhall, this similarity between how we relate to picture-objects – drawn faces, for example – and how we relate to "real"-objects – flesh and blood faces, for example – just is what Wittgenstein is calling 'continuous aspect perception' (cf. 2001, 253–4). I see no support for this interpretation in Wittgenstein's text. As I understand Wittgenstein, he is noting that our perceptual experiences with such picture-objects – including the experience of aspect-dawning – are *not unique* to such objects, and may also be had with "real" objects. So, on my reading, Wittgenstein is *downplaying* the representational function of picture-objects, not stressing it as key to the understanding of aspect perception, as Mulhall suggests. I argue at greater length against Mulhall's interpretation of these remarks in Baz 2000 and 2010.

"continuously seeing an aspect". *Grammatically*, the "aspect" here is an object of sight of Wittgenstein's *first* category.

Nor is there any particular *phenomenology* to the "continuous seeing" of an aspect as it is here described. Among other things, as we saw, the seeing of an aspect as elsewhere described by Wittgenstein is marked by a certain awareness that we play a role in what we see, that the aspect is not independent of us, and by an occupation with what we see – 'a paying of attention', as Wittgenstein says in one of his remarks (1992, 15). In contrast, the perceiver in the case of "continuous seeing" of an aspect might give her response to the question "What's that?" after a momentary glance at the drawing, hardly paying any attention to it beyond what is needed for recognizing it well enough to answer the question; and should the question come up again, she might very well give her answer without even looking at the drawing – after all, she takes herself to already know what the picture-object is.[37] Here we can begin to see the significance of conceptualizing what we perceive: it frees the object, so to speak, from its dependence on its perceivers, by situating it in the objective world, turning it into the potential object of a more or less useful piece of information that may be passed from one person to another.

There is perhaps no better way to see that 'continuous seeing of an aspect' is not simply a continuous version of what Wittgenstein elsewhere refers to as the 'seeing of an aspect' than to note that even the person he calls 'aspect-blind' should be perfectly capable of 'continuously seeing an aspect' as it is characterized in PPF 118–122. The aspect-blind is defined by Wittgenstein as someone who lacks 'the capacity to see something as something' (PPF, 257). And while it is not at all easy to understand such total incapacity,[38] for present purposes it is enough just to note that nothing Wittgenstein says about the aspect-blind should make us think he would be unable to tell a picture of a rabbit when he saw one; and I don't see why the person in PPF, 118–122, does anything more than just

---

[37] For this reason, "continuous seeing" is a little misleading as a translation of "*stetigen Sehe*" here; "constant" or "stable" might have been better, less misleading.

[38] Wittgenstein himself says that what is meant by "aspect blindness" stands in need of elucidation (PPF, 257). I was only able to truly make sense of "aspect-blindness" when I read Merleau-Ponty's description of Schneider, a patient of Gelb and Goldstein's, in the *Phenomenology of Perception* (cf. PP. 103ff). Schneider is incapable of creatively, playfully, *projecting* perceivable sense onto a given situation – unable to perceive a situation otherwise than how (some impersonal) "one" would perceive it, and unable to recognize and respond to ambiguity. And whereas for Wittgenstein the question of what, if anything, the aspect-blind might be missing is a difficult question for which he himself offers no very satisfying answer, Merleau-Ponty gives us detailed descriptions of all of the ways in which Schneider is different from the normal human perceiver. This, I have found, is one place where phenomenology is more enlightening than Wittgensteinian grammar.

that.[39] If the aspect-blind were unable to tell a picture of a rabbit when he saw one, his handicap would be way severer than "not being able to *see something as something*"; and, actually, it would then make no sense to attribute the latter to him.

But if even the *aspect-blind* is capable of "continuously seeing an aspect" as characterized by Wittgenstein, what justifies calling it "seeing an aspect" at all? It only makes sense to talk about "continuous seeing of an aspect" here, because *someone else*, who knows that there is another way to see this picture, 'could have said of me: "He is seeing the figure as a picture-rabbit"' (PPF, 121). The "seeing of an aspect" Wittgenstein is talking about here can be said to occur whenever *we* may say of *someone else* that she sees an object under a particular aspect, because she describes the object one way whereas *we* know that it could also be *seen*, and accordingly described, differently.[40] Now, of course, that person could maintain that description, offer it whenever asked what this object is, and so be said to continuously (constantly, stably) see an aspect, or see the object under one of its aspects. But it is an altogether different sense of "seeing an aspect" from the one it has in almost all of Wittgenstein's other remarks on aspect perception.

Moreover, "continuous seeing" of an aspect as here used by Wittgenstein is only applicable to ambiguous figures – or anyway to things we know may be seen in several, more or less determinate ways. It does not apply, for example, to the case Wittgenstein uses to introduce the concept of "(noticing an) aspect", of being struck all of a sudden by the similarity of one face to another – where one comes to see that other face in the face one is looking at, and the perceived physiognomy of the latter changes, and changes wholly. Here the dawning aspect has not replaced some other aspect under which that face had been seen up until the dawning of the similarity. We were seeing the face all right, but under no particular aspect. And if one wanted to insist that we were seeing the face continuously *as a face*, going against Wittgenstein's warnings that it makes no sense to talk of seeing something *as* what we *know* it to *be* (PPF, 122 and 203), it should then be noted that *that* "aspect" wasn't eclipsed by the dawning similarity – as the duck is eclipsed by the rabbit, and vice versa – which means that that other alleged "aspect" is not grammatically, or ontologically, on a par with the dawning aspect.

---

[39] Wittgenstein says about the aspect-blind that while he cannot – by definition, as it were – see one face *as* (similar to) another, he should 'be able to execute such orders as "Bring me something that looks like *this*!"'. And, similarly, while the aspect-blind cannot *see* the Necker cube *as* going this or that way, 'it would not follow from this that he could not recognize it as a representation (a working drawing, for instance) of a cube' (PPF, 258).

[40] We may also come to say some such thing about ourselves, in retrospect, when we realize that what we took to be an unambiguous picture of a duck, say, may also be seen as a rabbit.

In few (very few!) of his remarks, Wittgenstein thinks of senses in which aspects could be, or become, 'continuous'.[41] He does so, I believe, not because this is his main interest – he gives no indication whatsoever that it is – but because it is another way of bringing out the grammatical peculiarity of aspects. In general, Wittgenstein seems to be suspicious of the talk of "continuously seeing *x* as (some determinate) *y*", and reminds us that the mere fact that we *could* see, or *have* momentarily seen, something as something, does not mean that *whenever* we see it, we see it under some aspect or another (cf. PPF 189; and RPPI, 512 and 526). This will become important for us in Section 5, when we discuss perceptual indeterminacy and the tendency among philosophers to overlook it.

Elsewhere, Wittgenstein proposes that for an aspect to (come to) be 'continuous', it would need to be (or become), for the perceiver, a piece of (presumed) knowledge, as in the case he describes in PPF 118–122 – so it would need to become an object of sight of Wittgenstein's first category.[42] Wittgenstein further proposes that those who talk about "continuous aspect perception", or of "continuously seeing *x* as *y*", conflate *perceiving* something as something and *conceiving*, or *cognitively taking*, something in some way: the person who says 'I've always seen it *this* way' really means to say 'I have always conceived it *this* way (*Ich habe es immer so aufgefasst*)' (RPPI, 524; see also RPPII, 436).

There could perhaps be senses other than the one discussed in the *Investigations*, of "continuously seeing an aspect", and there is nothing wrong with exploring those senses,[43] as long as we keep in mind the sense of "seeing

---

[41] It's worth noting that in the English translations of Wittgenstein's remarks on aspects, "continuous" translates sometimes "*stetig*", sometimes "*dauernd*", and sometimes "*chronisch*", where each one of those German words is used in only a couple of remarks. That might encourage the idea that "continuous seeing" of an aspect is more central to Wittgenstein's remarks on aspects than it actually is, and that it always refers to the same thing in those remarks.

[42] Wittgenstein imagines, for example, someone saying that he is 'continuously seeing [some] figure red (*Ich sehe diese Figur dauernd rot*)' (1980a, 863). But "red" names a property of the object, which Wittgenstein contrasts with aspects (PPF, 247); and he also says that the person saying that just means that 'the description, that it is red ... is continuously correct (*dauernd richtig ist*)' (1980a, 863). Wittgenstein then says the same thing about continuously seeing one aspect of an ambiguous figure: ' ... that description, without any variation, is the right one and *that* only means that the aspect did not change' (1980a, 863–4). Thus, as we also saw in the case of the sole mentioning of "continuous seeing of an aspect" in section xi of the *Investigations*, one way in which the aspect can be seen "continuously" is by being, for the person seeing it, just something they (take themselves to) know about the object, and so something that person may be said to see in Wittgenstein's *first* sense of "see" (PPF, 111).

[43] Mulhall has made the notion of "continuous aspect perception" appear less problematic than it actually is, and more central to Wittgenstein's remarks, by equating "perceiving *x* as *y*" with "regarding *x* as *y*", or "treating *x* as *y*" (cf. 1990, 123). I was able to find only one remark potentially consonant with that interpretation. There, Wittgenstein says that 'in the chronic sense (*im chronischen Sinne*), the aspect is only the kind of way in which we again and again treat the picture (*die Figur behandeln*)' (1980a, 1022). But then he notes the grammatical difference

an aspect" for which there is no continuous version; for that is the sense of "seeing an aspect" that is primarily under grammatical investigation in Wittgenstein's remarks. The aspect can stay with us for some time, but cannot, grammatically, stay with us for long while remaining, for us, its perceivers, an *aspect*:

> If this constellation is always and continuously a face for me, then I have not named an aspect. For that means that I always encounter it as a face; whereas the peculiarity of the aspect is that I see something into a picture. So that I might say: I see something that isn't there at all, that does not reside in the figure, so that it may surprise me that I see it (at least, when I reflect upon it afterwards) (RPPI, 1028).

> There is a physiognomy in the aspect, which then fades away (PPF, 238).
> 'I noticed the likeness between him and his father for a few minutes, and then no longer' (PPF, 239).

> I should like to say that what dawns here lasts only as long as I am occupied with the object in a particular way [...] Ask yourself 'For how long am I struck by a thing?' – For how long is it *new* to me? (PPF, 237).

> If someone were to tell me that he had seen the figure for half an hour without a break as a reversed F, I'd have to suppose that he had kept on *thinking* of this interpretation, that he had *occupied* himself with it (RPPI, 1020).

> It is as if the aspect were something that only dawns, but does not remain; and yet this must be a conceptual remark, not a psychological one (RPPI, 1021).[44]

It looks as though readers of Wittgenstein's remarks on aspects have tended to suppose that what happens in the "dawning of an aspect" cannot be *that* different from what happens when we "continuously see" it. The latter is taken to be but an extended version of the former. 'The change of aspect in an ambiguous figure is simply the correlate of the unchanged aspect in an unam-biguous drawing', says Johnston (1993, 43). And Marie McGinn says, 'If we

---

between treating the picture in a certain way and seeing it under an aspect: 'The expression of the aspect is the expression of a way of taking (hence, of a way-of-dealing-with (*Behandlungsweise*), of a technique); but used as a description of a state' (RPPI, 1025, my emphases); and in another place, he says that 'the essential thing about seeing is that it is a state' (RPPII, 43). So in so far as an aspect stays with us by somehow becoming incorporated into the way we treat an object, or by becoming such a way – and with many Wittgensteinian aspects, it's not even clear what that would mean – it thereby ceases to be something that we can sensibly be said to *see*, at least in the sense in which Wittgensteinian aspects may be said to be seen. Shortly we shall see that when something does become incorporated into our habitual way of engaging with an object, Wittgenstein no longer wishes to call it "an *aspect*".

[44] In Section 5, I will propose that the necessary momentariness of the aspect is not just grammat-ical but also *phenomenological*. To perceive an aspect, you must attend to the object in a particular way; and, normally, we have limited control over what we attend to and how, and for how long.

feel disinclined to speak of "seeing" at all [in the case of the dawning of an aspect], then we should recall the connection with the case of continuous aspect seeing: in that case "It's a rabbit" is a straightforward perceptual report ... ' (1997, 192). Mulhall also makes the change from the dawning of an aspect to the continuous seeing of it seem very simple: the same words that in the dawning of an aspect serve as an *Äußerung*, as giving voice to the experience of having been struck by an aspect, are now employed 'as a simple perceptual report' (1990, 20). That, however, is to ignore both the grammar and the phenomenology of Wittgensteinian aspects, or to take neither as essential to what he means by "aspect".

It is only when one disregards the grammar and phenomenology of Wittgensteinian aspects, and focuses on the ambiguous figures and schematic drawings as encountered in the rather artificial context of the philosophy study or psychology lab – which makes it more likely that that grammar will not come into view and that the normal phenomenology will be distorted – that one can come to think that the aspect that dawns, and our perceptual relation to it, cannot be significantly different from the aspect that is "continuously seen", and our perceptual relation to *it*. This is not unlike supposing that there is no significant difference between falling in love with someone and loving that person all your life: in both cases, you love that person. But the criteria of each are *very* different from those of the other, and the latter is not simply an extended version of the former. Nor is the former a momentary experience of a shift in, or against the background of, the latter. To continuously see an aspect – where "seeing an aspect" is understood in the sense Wittgenstein is focusing on in his remarks – would be akin to continuously falling in love with the same person. And I'm not saying that either of those is entirely unimaginable. We just need to be clear on what it is we are trying to imagine.

5 Aspects and Perceptual Indeterminacy

I suspect that the argument of Section 4 will encounter resistance among the significant number of Wittgenstein's readers who have come to believe that there is, that there must be, a continuous version of the perception of aspects. It would likely be felt that even if the idea of continuous aspect perception is difficult to reconcile with much of what Wittgenstein says about what *he* calls 'aspects', that may be due to nothing more than the peculiarity of his use of that term. The idea itself, it would likely be felt, is surely right. For who would deny that most of what we lay our eyes on in the course of everyday experience – faces, flowers, bushes, trees, staircases, windows, books, laptops, knives and forks ... – is perfectly familiar to us and immediately recognizable as the particular (sort of) thing it is, and moreover presents us with a more or less familiar physiognomy? Call those familiar physiognomies 'aspects', or don't call them that, it might be argued, that would not change the plain truth to which those who have argued for continuous aspect perception have been trying to do justice.

I take this anticipated line of resistance seriously, and do not suppose that it may effectively be put to rest just by way of the deliberate assembling of Wittgensteinian grammatical reminders, let alone reminders concerning what *Wittgenstein* calls 'aspects'. In responding to this line of resistance, I will therefore put together some of the main points argued for in previous sections and considerations – mostly drawn from Merleau-Ponty's work – that go beyond anything I have found in Wittgenstein.

The key, as I see it, is the distinction between the phenomenal world – the world *as perceived and responded to* prior to being *thought*, or thought (or talked) *about* – and the world as objectively known (or taken to be known, or otherwise understood in objective terms), and the tendency to attribute to the former the sort of determinacy and independence-of-any-particular-perceiver that are characteristic of the latter. The dawning of Wittgensteinian aspects helps to bring into view the phenomenal world, and its distinction from the world as objectively known, or thought about. Whereas for Strawson and Wollheim the significance of aspect perception as described by Wittgenstein lies in giving us a way to cash out the idea that everything and anything we perceive is conceptualized, for me its significance lies pretty much in the opposite direction – namely, in bringing out the fundamental distinction between how we perceive something and how we conceive of it, or what we cognitively take it to be.

I have argued in Sections 2 and 3 that judging that one face *is* similar to another, or otherwise *conceiving* of a similarity between them, is one thing, having a similarity between them *perceptually dawn* on one is another. That distinction shows itself as well in the less natural cases of Wittgensteinian seeing-as. Thus, for example, it is one thing to (cognitively) take, or consider, the duck-rabbit drawing to be a picture of a duck (say), or to be meant to serve as such a picture, and quite another thing to *see* it *as* a duck. Similarly, it is one thing to (cognitively) take the Necker cube to (be meant to) represent a cube going *this* rather than *that* way, and quite another thing to be able to *see* it *as* going this or that way. As I've already noted, the former is something that even the 'aspect blind', as characterized by Wittgenstein, could do.

This distinction between our perceptual experience of something, or how it presents itself to us perceptually, and what we judge, or (take ourselves to) know it to objectively be, is not merely a grammatical or conceptual quirk, and is certainly not dependent on Wittgenstein's particular use of 'aspect'.[45] 'Ordinary experience', Merleau-Ponty writes, 'draws a clear distinction between sense experience and judgment' (PP, 34/35). He appeals to cases where we know, or think, one thing about what we perceive, but perceptually *experience* something else. One of those cases is that of the Necker cube:

> A cube drawn on paper changes its appearance accordingly as it is seen from one side and from above or from the other and from below. Even if I *know* that it can be seen in two ways, the figure in fact refuses to change its structure and my knowledge must await its intuitive realization. Here again one ought to conclude that judging is not perceiving (PP, 34/36).

As Wittgenstein notes, *seeing* something *as* something requires that you perceptually *attend to the object* in a particular way, and lasts only as long as you maintain that particular mode of attention. In Section 4, I proposed, following Wittgenstein, that it therefore could not be one's normal or habitual relation to the object, could not be *continuous* – not even if we *willed* it to be; for what we attend to and how, is not normally subject to the will, certainly not for long. What *could* be continuous is, precisely, a *cognitive* relation to an object – cognitively taking it to be one thing, or type of thing, or another (see RPPI, 524). Strawson is therefore right when he argues, following Kant, that it is only by way of the application of concepts that objects of perception acquire the sort of independence from any(one's) particular perceptual experience of them that situates them determinately in the objective world.[46] His mistake is to overlook the unity and sense, as well as the persistence and stability, that the world has for us at any given moment – however indeterminately – apart from the application of concepts. It is *that* level of perception, I am proposing, that the dawning of Wittgensteinian aspects brings out, not the level at which the phenomenal world becomes conceptualized.[47] The phenomenal world is 'the text', as Merleau-Ponty puts it, that 'our various forms of knowledge attempt to translate into precise language' (PP, xviii/lxxxii), as well as the milieu within which, and the background against which, those attempts acquire their sense for us.[48]

---

[45] Mulhall has correctly seen that the distinction between the perception of aspects and what Wittgenstein sometimes refers to as 'merely knowing (what the object is)' is central to Wittgenstein's understanding of aspects (cf. PPF, 169, 175, 180, and 192). I believe he spoiled the insight, however, by taking 'seeing aspects' to characterize all (normal, human) seeing, and by taking Wittgenstein's '(merely) knowing' to refer to a misguided 'metaphysical' *view* of human perception (cf. 1990, 19; and 2001, 253), thereby obscuring the fact that Wittgenstein is not operating here with 'technical vocabulary' (2001, 246), but rather is reminding us of a grammatical distinction that is perfectly familiar and commonplace.

[46] Strawson 1982, 87–8.

[47] Though, as I've already noted, the former level is the basis for the latter.

[48] It is, after all, one of Wittgenstein's most fundamental insights, and one that he shares with the phenomenological tradition, that what may sensibly be called "the application of concepts"

Those who have taken the continuous seeing of aspects to be unproblematic have tended to conflate the question of how you see something – how it organizes itself under your gaze, so to speak – and how you conceive of it, or what you take it objectively to be.[49] They have taken what we *know* (or take ourselves to know) we perceive – that is, objects of sight of Wittgenstein's first category, determinate objects determinately situated in the objective world – to determine what we actually perceive, in the sense of how things actually present themselves to us in our perceptual experience. They have, in effect, taken the world as objectively thought of and understood to be, or determine, the world *as perceived*. They have thus committed a version of what Merleau-Ponty, following Husserl and Gestalt psychologists, calls 'the experience error' (PP, 5/5). I'll say more about the experience error in the Appendix.

The dawning of Wittgensteinian aspects reveals the experience error to be indeed an error. It shows that there is a perceived physiognomic unity, or overall sense, that is importantly different from the unity, or overall sense, capturable in objective judgments (Kantian *Erkenntnisse*, Fregean *Gedanken*). It shows that the 'constancy hypothesis' is false (PP, 7/8): there is no one-to-one correlation between the world we objectively *know*, or *think*, we perceive, on the one hand, and the world *as perceived*, on the other hand.[50]

---

happens in a world that is already shared with others; and *that* world – the background ('form of life') apart from which our acts of conceptualization would not have whatever sense they have for us – cannot itself be conceptualized, our relation to *it* cannot be 'mediated by concepts', on pain of an infinite regress of conceptualization-of-the-background-of-conceptualization; and also, as I will later note, on pain of losing the figure-background structure that is essential to all perception, including the perception that issues in judgments.

[49] In Strawson and Wollheim, that conflation is explicit. In Mulhall, it is less obvious, since he proposes to cash out "continuous aspect perception" in terms of how we 'relate' to things, which he in turn connects with Heidegger's anti-intellectualist notion of "readiness-to-hand" (cf. 1990, 139–40; and 2001, 265). Even setting aside the difficulty posed for Mulhall's reading of Wittgenstein by the grammatical distinction, noted earlier, between how you treat or regard something and how you see it, there's the problem that "how one relates to something" is terribly vague; and on any natural understanding of it, it does not seem that there is any *one* particular way one relates to any of the things we encounter in the course of everyday experience: things encountered may well be ready-to-hand for us before becoming objects of knowledge, or true-or-false judgments, but, apart from this or that particular context of engagement, *not in any one particular way*. (A tree, for example, may offer shelter from the rain, or from the sun, or (if it is large enough) from bullets, or it may invite climbing, or serve as an anchor, or as something from which to hang a swing, or as something behind which to hide, or as a source of timber, or firewood, or it may just obstruct the view or block the path ...) So the Heideggerian notion of readiness-to-hand actually supports the idea of perceptual indeterminacy (which will soon be explained in further detail), and undermines the idea of continuous aspect perception. Mulhall avoids that difficulty, by cashing 'continuous aspect perception' out in terms of 'relating to an object as one particular *kind of object* or another' (2001, 265, my emphasis); and *that* is where his (tacit) conflation of perception and conception becomes evident.

[50] Merleau-Ponty borrows the notion of 'constancy hypothesis', as well as the idea that gestalt switches refute the hypothesis, from Wolfgang Köhler.

And it arguably shows more than that. Arguably, it shows, or at least helps to bring into view, that the world-as-perceived is characterized by irreducible *indeterminacy*. And it is that indeterminacy that the idea of continuous aspect perception seems to me to overlook, or cover up.

Early on in the *Phenomenology of Perception* Merleau-Ponty says that 'We must recognize the indeterminate as a positive phenomenon' (PP, 6/7) – that is, not as due to some kind of *contingent limitation* of our cognitive or perceptual powers. This is one of the most difficult ideas in his account of perception – difficult both to understand and to accept. I will not here attempt anything like a full explication and defense of that idea.[51] I do want to propose, however, that the dawning of Wittgensteinian aspects may be seen as an illustration of it, and as lending it support. And the basic point, as I see it, is actually fairly simple. The dawning of aspects reveals the role we play in effecting and sustaining the physiognomy – the perceived unity and sense - of what presents itself to us in perception, by attending to it in a particular way ('aspects are (to some extent) subject to the will'); I know no advocate of continuous-aspect-perception who denies that, and anyone who denied *that* would drain the notion of 'continuous *aspect* perception' of any sense. But if so, and since what we attend to perceptually in the normal course of everyday experience must have been perceived by us *prior* to our attending to it in some particular way – for otherwise, it could not have *drawn* our attention, or *invite* us to attend to it in a particular way – it follows that it had been perceived by us under no particular aspect, and was, in that sense, perceptually – or if you will aspectually – indeterminate.

This is likely to be missed, and has in fact been missed, by those who mostly focus on the deliberately ambiguous figures that are encountered in the artificial context of a philosophical illustration or psychological experiment. In the case of the duck-rabbit, for example, it seems just obvious that the determinate aspect that dawns replaces another, equally determinate aspect under which the object had been seen up until the dawning of the new aspect. Here it would help to remind ourselves of some of Wittgenstein's other examples of aspect dawning, such as the case we've discussed in which one is all of a sudden perceptually struck by the similarity of one face to another. In that case, as already noted in Section 4, there does not seem to be any plausible candidate for the competing aspect under which the face had been seen up until right before the dawning of the new aspect. We had been seeing the face all right, but not as having some particular, determinate overall expression or physiognomy – not unless we had been *struck*, for some time and right up until the dawning of the similarity, by

---

[51] In Baz (2017b), I do significantly more by way of explicating and motivating Merleau-Ponty's idea of perceptual indeterminacy.

some other expression or physiognomy. Nor, as already noted, would it help to insist here that we had been seeing the face continuously *as a face*; for, as Wittgenstein notes, that insistence makes no (clear) sense, and, in any case, *that* alleged 'aspect' does not disappear when the similarity aspect dawns.

Over-focusing on the duck-rabbit, the Necker cube, and other deliberately ambiguous figures that are attended to in the artificial setting of the philosophy study or classroom, or the psychology lab, might lead us to forget that the dawning of a Wittgensteinian aspect in the natural course of everyday experience – which is, after all, the 'natural home' of the concepts Wittgenstein investigates (PI, 116) – is not normally the replacement of one determinate physiognomy by another determinate physiognomy. Rather, it is the necessarily passing replacement of an indeterminate physiognomy with a *relatively* determinate one:[52] some particular way of *perceptually* taking hold of the object replaces, for a time, not (normally) some other particular way or taking hold of it, but rather no particular way of taking hold of it.

I have suggested that the dawning of an aspect may aptly be thought of as the *introduction* of a passing determinacy – a momentary perceptually-taking-hold of the object.[53] But now, is the *dawning* aspect determinate *while it lasts*? That would depend, of course, on what one means by 'determinate'. It is undeniable that in *some* cases we are readily able to describe the dawning aspect well enough to get other people to (see whether they can) see it. I note again that that is not always the case: sometimes aspects dawn on us for which we have no readily available description; something strikes us all of a sudden about the mood of a party, or the spirit of our time, for example, and we struggle to put it into words, and perhaps even find that someone else is better able to do so than we are. This may be one reason for feeling gratitude toward literature and poetry.[54] As Juliet Floyd notes, there are 'cases of aspect-perception [in which] there is a more open-ended range of significance:

---

[52] I say 'relatively', because, as I will later propose, aspects, at least those that dawn on us in the natural course of everyday experience, are always in principle open for, and sometimes may be found to call for, competing or further precisified articulations.

[53] That, according to Merleau-Ponty, is true of the perception of colors as well:

We must first understand that this red under my eyes is not as is always said, a *quale*, a pellicle of being without thickness, a message at the same time indecipherable and evident, which one has or has not received, but of which, if one has received it, one knows all there is to know, and of which in the end there is nothing to say. It requires a focusing, however brief; it emerges from a less precise, more general redness, in which my gaze was caught, into which it sank, before – as we put it so aptly –*fixing* it. And, now that I have fixed it, if my eyes penetrate into it, into its fixed structure, or if they start to wonder round about again, the *quale* resumes its atmospheric existence (Merleau-Ponty 1968, 131–2).

[54] In *Dora Bruder*, Patrick Modiano talks about how the German occupation of Paris and its horrors have been covered up, and for the most part forgotten. 'Nobody remembers anything anymore',

What is to be discerned is not an object or fact or concept, but a world, a human being, an expression or gesture, a total field of significance' (2010, 324). In Section 2 I said that cases of this kind are more clearly telling than others against the idea that whenever an aspect dawns on us there is some particular concept (or set of concepts) to which it corresponds.

Let us next look more closely at those cases in which we do seem to have a readily available description of the dawning aspect. With some of those cases – the Necker cube, for example, or the double cross – it's hard to think of a further determination of the aspect beyond that provided by its ready description ('The cube is oriented *that* way relative to me', or 'A white cross against a black background'). But as soon as we move to even slightly more complex objects and aspects, that is no longer true. Thus we may say that we see a similarity between one face and another, for example, or that we see the duck-rabbit as a duck, or as a rabbit. But surely, 'a similarity to some other, given face' does not capture the particular physiognomy that has dawned on us. And even the two aspects of the duck-rabbit, for all of their schematicity, may be found to have physiognomies – 'quite particular expressions', as Wittgenstein puts it in the *Brown Book* (BB, 135)[55] – that go beyond anything capturable by 'duck' and 'rabbit'.[56] (I would go as far as to propose the following: normal human perceivers cannot attend perceptually to a *face*, however schematic and however unlike a human face, without seeing it as expressive – however indeterminate its expression might be.)

We *could* try to *further* describe the dawning physiognomy. The duck, we might say, looks serious and somewhat self-important, like a retiring general posing for a portrait. The rabbit too looks pleased with itself, but in a more naïve or less pompous way, like a teenager driving an open-roofed convertible for the first time, taking pleasure in the feeling of freedom and speed and the wind in his hair, as well as in the thought of the (imagined) envious gazes of onlookers. (Similarly, we could try to describe the similarity – the shared physiognomy – we see between the faces. Or it could happen that the similarity strikes us, we call upon someone else to see it too, and then we find that the other is better able than we are to describe or articulate the similarity, the shared physiognomy.)

I wish to propose, however, that no description we might give of either of the duck-rabbit aspects (or of the shared physiognomy of two faces) would be

---

he writes. 'And yet', he goes on to say, 'from time to time, beneath this thick layer of amnesia, you can certainly sense something, an echo, distant, muted, but of what, precisely, it is impossible to say' (1999, 109).

[55] See also a note attached to *PI*, 165.

[56] In my own experience, even the letter F has a quite particular physiognomy when seen as facing right, and a very different physiognomy when seen as facing left. And in each case, the physiognomy goes beyond, is more specific than, whatever "facing right", or "facing left", may describe.

complete, unique, and final, in the sense that it could not be improved upon or contested. Someone else, or we at a later moment, could see the duck as loyal and eager to please but not too intelligent, for example, and the rabbit as stunned and taken aback by something it faces.[57] Each such description would only be an 'approximation', as Wittgenstein puts it (1958, 162); and *any* description of the aspect would be improvable, or contestable. In this respect too, such Wittgensteinian aspects are akin to Kantian beauty, which Kant at one point characterizes as 'a presentation of the imagination that compels (or even obliges, *veranlasst*) much thinking, but to which no determinate thought whatsoever, i.e. no concept, can be adequate' (2000, 314).

The phenomenon of aspect dawning, far from showing that everything we perceive is perceived under some determinate aspect or another, should therefore make us suspicious of that idea. Those who take the idea of continuous aspect perception to be clear and unproblematic, I have proposed, invariably conflate how we *see* something and how we *conceive* of it, or what we (take ourselves to) know it to be;[58] and then they attribute to the former the *relative* determinacy and stability that characterize the latter.[59]

But it's not just the conflation of how we perceive things and what we (take ourselves to) know them to be, and the over-focusing on schematic figures that are deliberately designed to be ambiguous, that are responsible for the widespread idea that whatever we perceive is perceived under some particular aspect or another, or perceived *as* some determinate this or that. Equally responsible for that idea, and equally problematic, is the tendency on the part of philosophers, and not just philosophers, to theorize about perception by reflecting on cases in which we are *already attending* perceptually to some more or less familiar object: an envelope (Moore), an apple (Grice), a yellow bush (Strawson), an oak tree (Wollheim), a red cube (McDowell), the duck-

---

[57] This illustrates the way in which the perceived physiognomy an object presents may change in accordance with its perceived, or imagined, background, which is one important source of perceptual indeterminacy.

[58] It is therefore unsurprising, perhaps, that Travis, who is very careful to distinguish between what presents itself to us in perception and what we judge it to be, or our conceptualization of it, has also denied that aspect perception, as characterized by Wittgenstein, characterizes normal human perception (cf. 2013, 102 and 180; and 2015, 45). And it's worth noting that the distinction Travis insists on, when coupled with his semantic 'contextualism' – the idea that the content expressible by sentences of the form 'This or that is such and such' depends in part on the context in which those sentences are used – implies that what presents itself to us in perception is *conceptually indeterminate*. My main disagreement with Travis concerns the fact that he methodically avoids saying anything about the world as perceived prior to, or apart from, our judging it to be some particular way or another. In Baz (2019), I argue that this methodical avoidance gets Travis into trouble when he attempts to account for the perception of Wittgensteinian aspects.

[59] I say 'relative', because even the determinacy of the objective world is historically conditioned and context-dependent. But that's a topic for another occasion.

rabbit . . . This makes it easy for them to forget that, *normally*, what we perceive belongs to a 'field' that is always organized into figure and background, and that we play a role in effecting that figure-background structure, by attending to something in a particular way and relegating other elements of the field to the background. Also forgotten is the question of what draws, or motivates, our attention, and how.

The attention-effected figure-background structure is not some contingent feature of normal human (and not just human) perception. It is an essential feature of it; and the fact that it has been neglected in so much philosophical theorizing about perception is therefore striking. 'Even if I knew nothing of rods and cones', Merleau-Ponty writes, 'I should realize that it is necessary to put the surrounding in abeyance the better to see the object, and to lose in background what one gains in focal figure [. . .]' (PP, 67–8/70). Moreover, as Merleau-Ponty notes (PP, 4/4, 6/6, and 13/13), and as empirical studies have shown, the background of what we attend to is not only indeterminate in its outline or shape,[60] but also indeterminate – or elements of the background are indeterminate – in any number of other respects (color saturation and hue, size, speed, contrast, and so on).[61] What lies in the background of what we attend to is perceived all right, but has no particular, determinate physiognomy for us.

This makes the idea of continuous aspect perception even more problematic than has hitherto emerged. The idea ignores altogether the dynamism of our perceptual field and of what we attend to and how. Is it plausible to think that (normal) human beings have some *one*, particular sort of perceptual relation, or 'attitude' (Mulhall 2001, 265), toward knives and forks, for example – a relation that holds *irrespective* of whether the perceiver is using the knife and fork for eating (while focusing on her food or on the conversation around the table), or is using them more or less creatively for some other purpose, or is setting the table, or is observing the setting of the table, or is setting the knife and fork aside, perhaps together with a bunch of other things, in order to make space for something else, or is examining the knife and fork for rust, or is having one's glance momentarily fall on the knife and fork, or is merely having them lie somewhere within one's field of vision

---

[60] See Köhler 1947, 107–8; and Baylis and Driver 1995.

[61] For empirical evidence – albeit evidence that relies on experiments conducted in very artificial perceptual settings – see Block 2010. It is interesting to note that Block argues in that paper that neither the position he calls 'realism' nor the position he calls 'representationalism' can do justice to the way attention affects our perceptual experience and, in particular, the perceptual indeterminacy of (what's in) the background. He is thereby repeating, in effect and in essence, the argument of chapter 3 of the 'Introduction' of the *Phenomenology of Perception*, in which Merleau-Ponty argues that neither 'empiricism' (Block's 'realism') nor 'intellectualism' (Block's 'representationalism') can do justice to the perceptual effects of attention.

while focusing on something else altogether? I think it is not plausible; and the empirical findings concerning the perceptual indeterminacy of what's in the background speak clearly against it. Nor is it plausible to think that the Heideggerian 'readiness-to-hand' of such objects, which Mulhall invokes in his interpretation of Wittgenstein (1990, 139–40; and 2001, 265), remains constant under any and all circumstances. It is only our knowledge of what these things objectively *are* that remains constant throughout such a range of perceptual experiences.

What we attend to and how is affected by any number of things. There are, first of all, practical motives: things may serve or hinder our practical aims in various ways under various circumstances, and may draw our attention in terms of their actual or potential practical significance; there are also addictions – to the screen, for example, or to certain contents available on screens, or else-where; or we play sports, or board-games, and elements on the field or on the board present themselves and call to our attention in terms of their significance to the game; and so on. And of course, our attention may also be drawn to things by other people, in any of those types of contexts, and in any number of ways – verbal and nonverbal.

Striking us with an aspect is another way in which things may draw, or hold, our attention. And one important respect in which aspect perception in the natural course of everyday experience is special is that, similarly to the experience of beauty as characterized by Kant, it is 'disinterested' (Kant 2000, 204–211). In contrast with all of the ways in which things attract and sustain our attention only in terms of, and insofar as they answer to, our pre-existing interests, in aspect perception no prior interest in the thing, or in anything else, is needed for drawing or sustaining our attention to it, and for giving sense to our calling upon others to share in our experience of it. The mere fact that we have been struck by something about the thing that has hitherto concealed itself from us, suffices for giving sense to, making intelligible, both our attending to the object in the way that we do and our attempting to share our experience with others.

6 The Significance of Aspect Perception

It has seemed obvious to many readers of Wittgenstein's remarks on aspect perception that the phenomenon of aspect dawning reveals something important about (normal, human) perception in general. For proponents of continuous aspect perception, the dawning of aspects reveals that we're always perceiving things under aspects, that anything and everything we (may be said to) perceive is perceived under some particular, determinate aspect or another; and aspect dawning is simply a switch from one such more or less extended perceptual relation to something to another. The main significance of aspect dawning is then taken to be that it makes us aware of our having always been in that perceptual relation to things – aspect perception – but without being aware of that, and precisely because the relation had been continuous. In Section 4, I argued against the attribution of some such idea to Wittgenstein. In Section 5, I offered phenomenological reasons for being suspicious of that idea. But while I believe the idea of continuous aspect perception bespeaks, at once, insufficient attention to Wittgensteinian grammar and lack of phenomenological sophistication, I don't think its proponents have been wrong in taking aspect dawning to have a broader significance and to be revelatory of normal human perception.

In a word, I think aspect dawning brings out the distinction between the phenomenal world – the world *as perceived and responded to* prior to being *thought*, or thought (or talked) *about* – and the objective world, or the world as objectively construed; and it reveals the role we play in bringing about and sustaining – 'constituting' as phenomenologists like to say – the unity and sense of the *former*.[62] Merleau-Ponty has taught us to understand this sort of pre-conceptual perceived synthesis in terms of *motor* and *affective* significance (see PP, 210ff./216ff.) – as unity and sense for *our phenomenal body*, first and foremost, not for our Kantian 'understanding', which is the faculty of concepts.[63]

---

[62] That we, together, play a role in bringing about and sustaining the unity and sense – the 'synthesis' – of the objective world is arguably Kant's most fundamental insight, and the heart of his critique of empiricism. What Kant missed in the *Critique of Pure Reason*, the phenomenologists have argued, and later, arguably, came to recognize when thinking about the experience of beauty, is the possibility of a synthesis that, while in some clear sense intelligible and intersubjectively shareable, is not (aptly thought of as) conceptual(ized) (see PP, xvii/lxxxi). The dawning of Wittgensteinian aspects, I have proposed, brings out especially clearly the distinction between the world-as-perceived and the world-as-objectively-construed, and the reality of intersubjectively shareable, perceived physiognomic synthesis that is not (yet) conceptually registered.

[63] The phenomenal body – the *lived*, or *living* body (*Leib*), as Husserl called it (Cf. 1970, 161 and 217–8) – is the body in its presence and availability to us prior to any theoretical reflection, and is to be distinguished from the body understood as an object of empirical study and objective cognition. The phenomenal body, be it our own or another person's, is a power and medium of actual and potential engagement with the phenomenal world: it is geared toward that world, takes hold of it in various ways, and responds to its solicitations. The phenomenal body and the phenomenal world are internally related to each other, in the sense that neither can be understood apart from its relation to the other: the phenomenal world is perceived as a field of actual and potential engagement by the phenomenal body; the phenomenal body is perceived as a power of actual and potential engagement with the phenomenal world. 'This subject-object dialogue', Merleau-Ponty writes, 'this drawing together, by the subject, of the meaning diffused through the object, and, by the object, of the subject's intentions … arranges around the subject a world which speaks to him of himself … ' (PP, 132/134; see also 441/465). That is the world that aspect perception helps to bring into view.

That the unity and sense of the aspect are not the unity and sense captured in concepts is something we've already seen in Section 2. The reference to the body may once again be harder to see in the case of schematic drawings that are detached from our perceptual field of actual and potential bodily engagement, and attended to in the artificial context of the study or lab. But even here, think about aspects such as *facing* or *pointing* right or left, being oriented *this* rather than *that* way in space (relative to me), being the *figure* (where something else is the background), which all make essential reference to the embodied perceiver. Aspects such as being the *conclusion*, being the *answer*, being the *introduction*, and so on, make sense to us only insofar as we are capable of *drawing conclusions*, *giving answers*, *introducing*, and so on, and of *responding* with understanding to other people's doing those things, and so once again make essential reference to our capacity for embodied engagement. And when we come to aspects such as the friendliness of a face, the slyness of a smile, the mood of the party, the beauty of a place or a sentence, and so on, the affective dimension of physiognomy becomes apparent as well. As I've noted in Section 5, even the duck and rabbit aspects of the duck-rabbit have an expressive, affective quality that goes beyond whatever 'duck' or 'rabbit' may capture.

Not only does the dawning of Wittgensteinian aspects reveal the role we play in creating and sustaining the sense we perceive, but it further reveals our capacity for more or less playful, more or less creative projection of perceivable sense onto some given object, or situation – what Merleau-Ponty refers to as the human being's 'genius for ambiguity' (PP, 189/195), and makes central to his phenomenological account of freedom. Freedom, for Merleau-Ponty, is the capacity to give meaning, or sense, to the situations in which we find ourselves that transcends their 'impersonal' meaning – the meaning they have for 'one' (Heidegger's '*Das Man*') (cf. PP, 450/475–6, and 453/480). It is, if you will, the capacity to perceive things and situations (and customs, and institutions) *anew*, and thereby contribute to the evolution of their perceived significance.

This gives us at once a way of understanding 'aspect-blindness' and an answer to Wittgenstein's question of what consequences aspect-blindness would have (PPF, 257). The aspect-blind person, I'm proposing, would be someone lacking in the capacity to project sense creatively, playfully – to perceive given things and situations otherwise than how 'one' would perceive them, or otherwise than what she objectively knows them to be. Schneider, the patient of Goldstein and Gelb whose case is central to Merleau-Ponty's exposition of the phenomenological perspective, is such an aspect-blind, incapable of creative sense-projection, of play-acting (PP, 104–5/107, and

135/136), and in that sense lacking in freedom, or 'productive power' (PP, 112/115, and 135/136): he is 'confined to the actual' as impersonally perceived (PP, 109/111, and 135/136), and his world is correlatively perceived as 'ready-made or congealed', lacking the indeterminacy and open-ended potentiality that characterizes the world of the normal perceiver (PP, 112/115). Aspect-blindness, thus understood, characterizes many on the autistic spectrum; but really, each one of us is somewhere on the spectrum of freedom and confinement – each more or less creative, playful, capable of seeing things anew. And it is also not uncommon to see someone who is capable of considerable creativity in certain areas or moments, but shows confinement or rigidity in others.

In the *Phenomenology of Perception*, Merleau-Ponty invokes the distinction between a problem and a riddle, and says that Schneider – the aspect-blind – cannot tell the difference between the two (PP, 135/136). A problem is *determinate*, in the sense that finding a solution to it does not change your perception or understanding of it. A riddle, by contrast, is *indeterminate* until solved: until you find the solution – or *a* solution– you do not really know what it is asking or calling for. The riddle and its solution come clearly and determinately into view – to the extent that they do – together. Cora Diamond, in whose interpretation of Wittgenstein the notion of the riddle plays a central role, puts the same basic point this way: 'It is only when one has the solution that one knows how to take the question, what it is for it to have an answer' (1991, 263). (I note that the line between problems and riddles, thus understood, is not sharp. Moreover, to the extent that a solution to what first presented itself as a problem does change our perception and understanding of it, it has revealed it as a riddle, in Merleau-Ponty's sense. In other words, whether a situation we face is a problem or a riddle is itself, partly, a matter of how we perceive and respond to it.)

For the aspect-blind, there are only problems, no riddles. Normal perception and (hence) behavior, Merleau-Ponty suggests, move somewhere in between riddle solving – finding answers to 'questions which are obscurely formulated' (PP, 214/222) – and problem solving. The freer, more personal and creative we are in how we perceive and respond to a situation in which we find ourselves, the more our perception of, and response to, that situation resemble riddle solving. The capacity to see aspects, I'm proposing, is tied to the capacity to perceive given situations in their indeterminacy, or ambiguity – to perceive them as riddles – and to come up with creative solutions or answers to them. But it would be hard to arrive at this sort of understanding of aspect-blindness and its significance just on the basis of Wittgensteinian grammatical reminders.

Appendix
The Natural Attitude and the Limitations of the Wittgensteinian Grammatical Investigation

Whereas many readers have tended to attribute to Wittgenstein a comprehensive, unified, and more or less complete 'view' of aspect perception, I see no support for this in his numerous remarks on the topic. Nor do I find any indication that he managed to arrive at some other sort of satisfying dissolution of the difficulties he encountered in this area. Witness his saying to Maurice Drury, not long before his death and after many years of thinking about aspect perception: 'Now try and say what is involved in seeing something as something; it is not easy. These thoughts I am now having are as hard as granite'.[64] Another area of difficulty with which Wittgenstein was grappling in his final years – and once again without arriving at anything like a satisfying dissolution of the difficulties – has to do with our relation to the background apart from which what we say (and think, and do, and feel) would not have the sense it has for us.[65] In both areas, the questions with which Wittgenstein grapples *are* difficult; and though they give rise to plenty of conceptual confusion and entanglement, I don't see them as rooted in conceptual confusion or entanglement. The basic difficulty in both areas, as I see it, is just the difficulty of phenomenology – the difficulty of bringing out and elucidating, without *thereby* distorting, what is, normally and in essence, not attended to, reflected upon, or articulated.

I want to propose, however, that Wittgenstein's struggles in these two areas – hereafter I will focus only on his difficulties with aspects – reveal not only the inherent difficulty of phenomenology, but also inherent limitations of his method of grammatical investigation. Wittgenstein's method, or set of related methods, is designed to enable us to overcome philosophical difficulties that arise when 'language goes on holiday' (PI, 38) – that is, when we rely on our words to express thoughts, or to otherwise carry determinate commitments or implications (determinate enough, in any case, for generating and sustaining precisely those philosophical difficulties), even apart from *our* meaning them in some determinate way or another, in a context suitable for meaning them that way. In the face of philosophical difficulties *thus* generated, the best response may well be therapy by way of the deliberate assembling of 'reminders' that aim at leading the words of our philosophizing 'back from their metaphysical to their everyday use' (PI, 116),

---

[64] Quoted in Monk 1991, 537.

[65] Wittgenstein's work on that issue, or set of issues, is well represented in the remarks collected in Wittgenstein 1969. Once again, I find Wittgenstein much farther from 'complete clarity' (PI, 133) in this area than many of his readers have taken him to be. I discuss Wittgenstein's difficulties in this area, as I see them, in Baz 2018.

thereby revealing the difficulties as difficulties with '*Luftgebäude*' (PI, 118) that are sustained by unreasonable and ultimately nonsensical expectations that we have of those words, and by pictures that encourage and sustain those expectations.

The basic problem, as I see it, for the Wittgensteinian grammatical investigation vis á vis phenomenology in general and aspect perception in particular, is the tendency of our ordinary and normal employment of words to be focused on capturing and objectifying – well enough for present intents and purposes – the world that comes into view in perception, rather than on our perceptual *experience* of that world. It is for that reason that reminders about the ordinary and normal employment of our words will only take us so far in phenomenology, and *might* actually lead us astray.

In its tendency to bypass our perceptual experience in favor of its objects, our ordinary and normal employment of words participates in what Merleau-Ponty, following Husserl, refers to as our 'natural attitude'. The natural attitude, according to Husserl, is that of being "immersed naively in the world" and "accept[ing] the experienc*ed* as such" (1998, 14, my emphasis) – focusing on "objects, values, goals," rather than "on the experienc*ing* of [one's] life" (1998, 15; see also 1970, 119 and 144). Husserl's "bracketing," or *epoché*, is meant to counteract our tendency to focus on the objects of perception, as objectively thought about and understood, and to overlook our experiencing of them – to overlook, that is, how those objects actually present themselves to us, and how we relate to them, before we begin to reflect on and theorize about perception from the perspective of the natural sciences, and therefore on the basis of what we take ourselves to already know, objectively, about what we perceive and about our perceptual apparatus.

Merleau-Ponty invokes the 'natural attitude' and the difficulty it creates for the phenomenologist when he says, in the Preface to the *Phenomenology of Perception*, that 'our existence is too tightly held in the world to be able to know itself as such at the moment when it is thrown into the world' (PP, xv/ lxxviii). He comes back to that idea early in the first chapter of that book, when he says that 'we are caught up in the world and ... do not succeed in extricating ourselves from it' (PP, 5/5). This natural involvement with the world, which Merleau-Ponty later refers to as our 'obsession with being' (PP, 70/73), culminates in the constitution of an objective world, which (failing to heed Kant's warnings!) we tend to think of as 'a world in itself' (PP, 41/43) – fully and finally determinate, and wholly independent of our experience of it (cf. PP, 47/48).

The main obstacle to understanding perception, and hence behavior, Merleau-Ponty argues, is the tendency to take the objective world – that is, the world as objectively construed – as the starting point in our theorizing about perception. In trying to reconstruct perception on the basis of what we take ourselves to already know objectively, we commit what Merleau-Ponty, following Köhler, calls 'the experience error': 'we make perception out of things perceived ... And since perceived things themselves are obviously accessible only through perception, we end up understanding neither' (PP, 5/5). 'Our perception,' he similarly says later on, 'ends in objects, and the object once constituted, appears as the reason for all the experience of it which we have had or could have' (PP, 67/69). The task of phenomenology, Merleau-Ponty writes, is therefore 'to rediscover phenomena, the layer of living experience through which other people and things are first given to us, the system of "self-others-things" as it comes into being; to reawaken perception and foil its trick of allowing us to forget it as a fact and as perception in the interest of the object which it presents to us and of the rational tradition to which it gives rise' (PP, 57/57).[66]

Now, if it is of the essence of normal perception to overlook itself in the interest of the object which it presents us – if, in other words, we do not perceive perception, do not perceptually attend to our perceptual relation to whatever it is we are perceiving and to the background against which we attend to it perceptually, and against which it has whatever sense it has for us – then it is only to be expected that our ordinary and normal use of words would participate in, and reflect, that overlooking of our pre-reflective perceptual experience. And if so, then there is reason to worry that the Wittgensteinian grammatical investigation, insofar as it takes its bearing from the ordinary and normal use of our words, will only take us so far when it comes to elucidating non-objective, or non-objectivized, perceptual experience. And it might lead us astray, by encouraging us to take the objective, or objectivizing, senses of our words as primary, and to commit the experience error.

Wittgenstein himself sometimes commits the experience error in his later writings, when he engages critically with the ideas of Gestalt psychologists (cf. RPPI, 1035; and RPPII, 474).[67] This comes out most clearly when he responds to Köhler's idea that when figure and background switch for us as we look at figures such as the 'double-cross', lines that we previously saw as 'belonging together' are no longer seen as 'belonging together', and vice versa.[68] Wittgenstein protests

---

[66] In a working note for *The Visible and the Invisible*, Merleau-Ponty similarly remarks that 'the temptation to construct perception out of the perceived, to construct our contact with the world out of what it has taught us about the world, is quasi-irresistible' (1968, 156). And then he adds that 'It is the inverse route we have to follow; it is starting from perception and its variants, described as they present themselves, that we shall try to understand how the universe of knowledge could be constructed' (1968, 157).

[67] Nomy Eilan has recently proposed, and has on good evidence taken Wittgenstein to propose, that "seeing" in the first sense mentioned in PPF 111 comes first, not only in the order of acquisition and use, but also in the order of perception – that the Wittgensteinian aspect merely 'overlays the physical object, as seen, and its apparent shape and colours' (2013, 9).

[68] See Köhler 1947, 100–1 and 108. My aim here is not to defend Köhler – I might be reading him *too* charitably (by my lights) – but to underscore the limitations of Wittgenstein's grammatical investigation.

that Köhler's account is misleading, because '[...] the radii that belonged together before belong together now as well; only one time they bound an 'arm', another time an intervening space' (RPPI, 1117). But, as Merleau-Ponty notes early on in the *Phenomenology of Perception* (PP, 4/4) and as empirical studies have shown,[69] we *actually do perceive* the outline of the figure we focus on as *belonging to the figure*, and *not* to its background (or intervening space), whose shape is *perceptually indeterminate* (cf. PP, 13/13);[70] and this, despite the fact – of which Köhler was well aware! – that when we consider the matter *objectively*, the outline of the figure is equally the outline of its background. Köhler was not forgetting or ignoring the objective, or objectivist, perspective. He was *challenging* the tendency, to which Wittgenstein has here succumbed, to take it as the starting point when attempting to describe and understand the world *as pre-reflectively perceived*.[71]

I have mentioned, in Section 1, Wittgenstein's mistrust of phenomenology, as it manifests itself in his remarks on aspects. I've also noted that his grammatical approach is an effective and well-motivated approach when it comes to the sort of philosophically troublesome concepts that are the focus of the first part of the *Investigations*: 'learning', 'understanding', 'meaning', 'naming', 'thinking', 'reading', 'intending', and so on. When it comes to concepts such as *those*, the attempt to elucidate them by way of reflection on the experiences we undergo when we learn, understand, think, intend, and so on, is bound to lead us astray. Here, what is needed is what Cavell has insightfully called Wittgenstein's 'undoing of the psychologizing of psychology' (1969, 91). However, when we wish, not to disentangle conceptual entanglements, but to bring out and elucidate our pre-reflective perceptual *experience*, and the world *as pre-reflectively perceived and responded to*, we need, at the very least, to supplement the Wittgensteinian method of grammatical investigation that proceeds on the basis of 'reminders' (PI, 127) of the 'kind of statements we make about phenomena' (PI, 90). For we do not normally make statements about our pre-reflective, perceptual experience; and even words that might be thought to refer us to that experience – 'see', 'hear', 'feel', 'notice', and so on – are not normally used for describing, or expressing, that experience. On the common, 'primary' use of 'see', for example – that's Wittgenstein's 'first use' of the word

---

[69] Köhler gives evidence for that in 1947, 108. For more recent empirical evidence, see Baylis and Driver 1995.

[70] See also Köhler 1947, 107.

[71] Cf. Köhler 1947, 55. In the Appendix to Baz 2017a, I argue that while the first use of 'see' Wittgenstein describes in PPF, 111, *is*, grammatically, primary, in the sense that it is acquired first and that you couldn't acquire the second use he describes – that is, the "seeing" of aspects – if you didn't already master the first, the second use of "see" refers us to what is *phenomenologically* primary, primary *in the order of perception*.

(PPF, 111) – what someone saw, is, as Travis has noted, mostly a matter of what was there anyway, objectively, to be seen.[72]

I am not saying that the difficulty of phenomenology may not, in principle, be overcome, or that our language somehow prevents us, in principle, from overcoming it. The work of phenomenology might be never-ending (see PP, xiv/lxxviii), but it is not impossible. Our words *may* be used for describing, or expressing, our perceptual experience, and the world as it presents itself to us prior to being thought or talked about. That our words may thus be used is itself part of the grammar of our language, and therefore part of what the Wittgensteinian grammatical investigation may bring out. The 'second use' of 'see' Wittgenstein describes, for example, refers us, precisely, to a particular sort of perceptual experience – namely, that of noticing, or being struck by, an aspect.

Still, it is one thing to bring out and elucidate the grammar of the phenomenological use of our words and its differences from their objectivizing, or object-oriented, uses, and another thing to *do phenomenology*, just as it is one thing to bring out and elucidate the grammar of empirical science, for example, or of aesthetic evaluation, and quite another thing to engage in empirical science, or in aesthetic evaluation. And what I've proposed is, first, that aspect perception gives rise to questions that are best answered by way of phenomenology, and, second, that Wittgenstein's grammatical investigation suffers limitations in *that* area.

To be clear, it is open to Wittgenstein, just as it is open to Merleau-Ponty and to everyone else, to try to *describe* our perceptual experience, and the world as it presents itself to us prior to becoming the object of true or false judgments.[73] And that, as we've seen, is something Wittgenstein does in some of his remarks. It should first of all be noted, however, that in order to do phenomenology *well* one needs to do more than just recognize pre-objective, pre-conceptual perceptual experience and attempt to describe it (as many people do, at least to some extent and more or less successfully, in the course of everyday life).[74] But, beyond that, my basic point is just that when Wittgenstein does attempt to

---

[72] See Travis 2013, 102 and 411; see also Travis 2015, 47.

[73] The *Phenomenology of Perception* is full of such descriptions: for example, when Merleau-Ponty describes the human subject as sustaining round about her 'a system of meanings whose reciprocities, relationships, and involvements do not require to be made explicit in order to be exploited' (PP, 129/131), or when he talks of the phenomenal body as 'rising toward the world' (PP, 75/78), or talks of the hand when used for touching something as 'shoot[ing] across space to reveal the external object . . . ' (PP, 92/94), or talks of our phenomenal body, when we lean with our hands against a desk, as trailing behind our hands 'like the tail of a comet' (PP, 100/102). As I go on to note in the text, it is of the essence of phenomenology that the phenomenologist will need to use his or her words creatively, as Merleau-Ponty does in such passages.

[74] I say more about Merleau-Ponty's method of investigation in the Appendix to Baz 2017a. Importantly, Merleau-Ponty's investigation proceeds on the basis of careful examination of a wealth of empirical findings concerning normal and abnormal perception and behavior – the sort of examination that is almost entirely absent from Wittgenstein's later work.

describe pre-reflective and pre-objective perceptual experience, he is no longer engaged in the grammatical investigation of philosophically troublesome words or concepts by way of the perspicuous representation of language-games, but rather is moving, as Cavell puts it, 'to regions of a word's use which cannot be assured or explained by an appeal to its ordinary language games' (1979, 189).

If, as I have proposed, the primary uses, hence meanings, of our words tend to partake of the natural attitude and to focus, or focus us, on objects and their objective constellations, rather than on our perceptual experience and the way things present themselves to us prior to becoming the objects of true-or-false judgments, then it is only to be expected that the phenomenologist will need to use her words creatively – in what Wittgenstein calls their 'secondary meanings'.[75] This, if you will, is part of the Wittgensteinian grammar of 'phenomenology'. But what it means is that when it comes to the work of phenomenology, one's philosophical footing is not going to be secured by reminding oneself how one's words are used 'in the language which is their original home' (PI, 116). That a displaced piece of furniture is no longer what it was prior to the displacement, for example, or that everything is part and parcel of everything else, or that the rhythm of our language, of our thinking and feeling is part of the background for our understanding of music, is not a piece of Wittgensteinian grammar, but rather a piece of what may aptly be called 'perceptual grammar'. When it comes to the work of phenomenology, one still needs to avoid the 'metaphysical' – empty, idle – use of one's words, if one wishes to make real progress; but leading those words *back* to their everyday use (PI, 116) is not going to satisfy one's real need in that area.

---

[75] Köhler, it should be noted in this connection, proposes that in order to do justice to our perception we would need *new concepts*, such as the *phenomenal* concepts of 'belonging together' and 'organization' (cf. 1947, 80). And Merleau-Ponty, whose creative use of words in the *Phenomenology of Perception* I have already noted, speaks in *The Visible and the Invisible* of the phenomenological 'effort that uses the significations of words to express, beyond themselves, our mute contact with the things, when they are not yet things said' (1968, 38).

References

Agam-Segal, R. (2019). 'Avner Baz on Aspects and Concepts: A Critique'. *Inquiry.* https://doi.org/10.1080/0020174X.2019.1610049

Austin, J. L. (1999). *How to Do Things With Words.* Cambridge, MA: Harvard University Press.

Baylis, G. C. and Driver, J. (1995). 'One-sided edge assignments in vision: figure-ground segmentation and attention to objects'. *Current Directions in Psychological Science* **4**(5): 140–146.

Baz, A. (2000). 'What's the Point of Seeing Aspects?'. *Philosophical Investigations* **23**(2): 97–121.

(2003). 'On When Words are Called For: Cavell, McDowell, and the Wording of Our World', *Inquiry* **46**(4): 473–500.

(2010). 'On Learning from Wittgenstein, or What Does it Take to *See* the Grammar of Seeing Aspects?'. In *Seeing Wittgenstein Anew.* Day, W. and Krebs, V. (eds.). New York: Cambridge University Press: 227–248.

(2011). 'Aspect Perception and Philosophical Difficulty'. In *Oxford Handbook of Wittgenstein*, Marie McGinn and Oskari Kuusela (eds.). New York: Oxford University Press: 697–713.

(2012). *When Words are Called For.* Cambridge, MA: Harvard University Press.

(2017a). *The Crisis of Method in Contemporary Analytic Philosophy.* New York: Oxford University Press.

(2017b). 'Motivational Indeterminacy'. *European Journal of Philosophy* **25**(2): 336–57.

(2018). 'Wittgenstein and the Difficulty of What Normally Goes Without Saying'. In *Language, Form(s) of Life, and Logic: Investigations after Wittgenstein.* Martin, C. (ed.). New York: de Gruyter: 253–276.

(2019). 'Bringing the Phenomenal World into View'. In *Wittgenstein on Objectivity, Intuition, and Meaning.* James Conant and Sebastian Greve (eds.). New York: Cambridge University Press: 100–118.

(2020). *The Significance of Aspect Perception: Bringing the Phenomenal World into View.* New York: Springer.

Bloom, P. (2000). *How Children Learn the Meanings of Words.* Cambridge, MA: MIT Press.

Block, N. (2010). 'Attention and Mental Paint'. *Philosophical Issues* **20**(1): 23–63.

(2014). 'Seeing-As in the Light of Vision Science'. *Philosophy and Phenomenological Research* **89**(3): 560–72.

Cavell, S. (1969). *Must We Mean What We Say?* New York: Cambridge University Press.

(1979). *The Claim of Reason.* New York: Oxford University Press.

Diamond, C. (1991). *The Realistic Spirit.* Cambridge, MA: MIT University Press.

Eilan, N. (2013). 'On the Paradox of Gestalt Switches: Wittgenstein's Response to Kohler'. *Journal for the History of Analytic Philosophy* **2**(3): 1–19.

Floyd, J. (2010). 'On Being Surprised: Wittgenstein on Aspect-Perception, Logic, and Mathematics. In *Seeing Wittgenstein Anew.* Day, W. and Krebs, V. (eds.). New York: Cambridge University Press: 314–337.

Frege, G. (1956). 'The Thought'. *Mind* **65**(259): 289–311.

Frege, G. (1999). *The Foundations of Arithmetic.* Austin, J. L. (trans.). Evanston, IL: Northwestern University Press.

Geach, P. (1965). 'Assertion'. *Philosophical Review* **74**(4): 449–465.

Grice, P. (1989). *Studies in the Way of Words.* Cambridge, MA: Harvard University Press.

Husserl, E. (1970). *The Crisis of the European Sciences and Transcendental Phenomenology.* David Carr (trans.). Evanston, IL: Northwestern University Press.

Husserl, E. (1998). *The Paris Lectures.* Koestenbaum, P. (trans.). Norwell, MA: Kluwer Academic Publishers.

Johnston, P. (1993). *Wittgenstein: Rethinking the Inner.* New York: Routledge.

Kant, I. (1998). *Critique of Pure Reason.* Guyer, P. and Wood, A. (trans.). New York: Cambridge University Press.

Kant, I. (2000). *Critique of the Power of Judgment.* Paul Guyer (ed.), Paul Guyer and Eric Matthews (trans.). New York: Cambridge University Press.

Koffka, K. (1927). *The Growth of the Mind: An Introduction to Child-Psychology* (second edition), M. R. Ogden (trans.). New York: Harcourt, Brace & Co.

Köhler, W. (1947). *Gestalt Psychology: An Introduction to New Concepts in Modern Psychology.* New York: Liveright.

McGinn, M. (1997). *Wittgenstein and the Philosophical Investigations.* New York: Routledge.

McGinn, M. (2010). 'Wittgenstein and Internal Relations', *European Journal of Philosophy* **18**(4): 495–509.

54

References

Merleau-Ponty, M. (1968). *The Visible and the Invisible*. Lefort, C. (ed.), and Lingis, A. (trans.). Evanston, IL: Northwestern University Press.

Merleau-Ponty, M. (1996/2012). *Phenomenology of Perception*. Colin Smith (trans.)/Donald Landes (trans). New York: Routledge.

Modiano, P. (1999). *Dora Bruder*. Kilmartin. J. (trans.). Berkeley, CA: University of California Press.

Monk, R. (1991). *Ludwig Wittgenstein: The Duty of Genius*. New York: Penguin Books.

Mulhall, S. (1990). *On Being in the World: Wittgenstein and Heidegger on Seeing Aspects*. New York: Routledge.

(2001). 'Seeing Aspects'. In *Wittgenstein: A Critical Reader*. Glock, H-J (ed.). Oxford: Blackwell.

Munro, A. (1996). *Selected Stories*. New York: Random House.

Schroeder, S. (2010). 'A Tale of Two Problems: Wittgenstein's Discussion of Aspect Perception', in J. Cottingham & P.M.S. Hacker (eds.), *Mind, Method, and Morality: Essays in Honour of Anthony Kenny*. New York: Oxford University Press: 352–371.

Searle, J. (1999). *Speech Acts*. New York: Cambridge University Press.

(2015). *Seeing Things as They Are: A Theory of Perception*. New York: Oxford University Press.

Strawson, P. (1982). 'Imagination and Perception'. In *Kant on Pure Reason*. Ralph Charles Sutherland Walker (ed.). New York: Oxford University Press: 82–99. (Originally published in *Experience and Theory*, Foster and Swanson (eds.). Amherst, Mass. and London: University of Massachusetts Press and Duckworth, 1971.)

Travis, C. (2013). *Perception*. New York: Oxford University Press.

(2015). 'Suffering Intentionally?'. In *Wittgenstein and Perception*. Campbell, M. and O'Sullivan, M. (eds.). New York: Routledge: 45–62.

Wittgenstein, L. (1958). *The Blue and Brown Books*. Oxford: Basil Blackwell.

(1969). *On Certainty*. Anscombe, G. E. M. and von Wright, G. H. (eds.). Anscombe, G. E. M. (trans.). New York: Harper and Row.

(1980a). *Remarks on the Philosophy of Psychology*, Vol. I, G. E. M. Anscombe and G. H. von Wright (eds.), tr. G. E. M. Anscombe. Oxford: Basil Blackwell.

(1980b). *Remarks on the Philosophy of Psychology*, Vol. II, G. E. M. Anscombe and G. H. von Wright (eds.), tr. C. G. Luckhardt and M. A. E. Aue. Oxford: Basil Blackwell.

(1980c). *Culture and Value*, G. H. von Wright (ed.), Winch, P. (tr.). Chicago, IL: The University of Chicago Press.

(1982). *Last Writings on the Philosophy of Psychology*, Vol. I, G. H. von Wright and H. Nyman (eds.), tr. C. G. Luckhardt and M. A. E. Aue (Chicago: University of Chicago Press).

(1983). *Lectures and Conversations on Aesthetics, Psychology and Religious Belief*, Cyril Barrett (ed.). Oxford: Basil Blackwell.

(1992). *Last Writings on the Philosophy of Psychology*, Vol. II, G. H. von Wright and H. Nyman (eds.), tr. C. G. Luckhardt and M. A. E. Aue. Oxford: Blackwell.

(2001). *Tractatus Logico-Philosophicus*. Pears, D. and McGuinness, B. (trans.). New York: Routledge.

(2009a). *Philosophical Investigations*, Part I, G. E. M. Anscombe, P. M. S. Hacker and Joachim Schulte (trans.). Malden, MA: Basil-Blackwell.

(2009b). *Philosophical Investigations*, Part II, G. E. M. Anscombe, P. M. S. Hacker and Joachim Schulte (trans.). Malden, MA: Basil-Blackwell, 2009.

Wollheim, R. (1980). *Art and Its Objects* (second edition). New York: Cambridge University Press.

Acknowledgments

Over the years I have benefited immeasurably in my work on aspect perception from criticisms and encouragement (often, both at once) from the following individuals: Reshef Agam-Segal, Stanley Cavell, Jim Conant, Bill Day, Dan Dennett, Juliet Floyd, Eli Friedlander, Razi Goren, Keren Gorodeisky, Sebastian Sunday Gréve, Martin Gustafsson, Arata Hamawaki, Jonah Horwitz, Peter Hylton, Kelly Jolley, Gary Kemp, Victor Krebs, Oskari Kuusela, Leonard Linsky, Christian Martin, Marie McGinn, Michael Mitchell, Stephen Mulhall, Jean-Philippe Narboux, and Charles Travis. I thank them all.

Cambridge Elements ≡

The Philosophy of Ludwig Wittgenstein

David G. Stern
University of Iowa

David G. Stern is a Professor of Philosophy and a Collegiate Fellow in the College of Liberal Arts and Sciences at the University of Iowa. His research interests include history of analytic philosophy, philosophy of language, philosophy of mind, and philosophy of science. He is the author of *Wittgenstein's Philosophical Investigations: An Introduction* (Cambridge University Press, 2004) and *Wittgenstein on Mind and Language* (Oxford University Press, 1995), as well as more than 50 journal articles and book chapters. He is the editor of *Wittgenstein in the 1930s: Between the 'Tractatus' and the 'Investigations'* (Cambridge University Press, 2018) and is also a co-editor of the *Cambridge Companion to Wittgenstein* (Cambridge University Press, 2nd edition, 2018), *Wittgenstein: Lectures, Cambridge 1930–1933, from the Notes of G. E. Moore* (Cambridge University Press, 2016) and *Wittgenstein Reads Weininger* (Cambridge University Press, 2004).

About the Series

This series provides concise and structured introductions to all the central topics in the philosophy of Ludwig Wittgenstein. The Elements are written by distinguished senior scholars and bright junior scholars with relevant expertise, producing balanced and comprehensive coverage of the full range of Wittgenstein's thought.

Cambridge Elements ☰

The Philosophy of Ludwig Wittgenstein

Printed in the United States
By Bookmasters